Beat the Bumph!

Cut Clutter,
Read Rapidly
and Succeed in the
Information Jungle

Kathryn M. Redway

NICHOLAS BREALEY
PUBLISHING
LONDON

Also by Kathryn Redway
Rapid Reading

First published in Great Britain by
Nicholas Brealey Publishing Limited in 1995
21 Bloomsbury Way
London WC1A 2TH

ISBN 1–85788–110–9 (hardback)
ISBN 1–85788–111–7 (paperback)

British Library Cataloguing in Publication Data
A catalogue record for this book is available from the
British Library.

Printed and bound in Finland by Werner Söderström Öy

Foreword

by *Tony Buzan*

Author of *Use Your Head* and *The Mind Map Book*

During my days at university I began to realise, with increasing alarm, that I was being inexorably buried underneath the growing mound of information that I was required to learn. One day, filled with hope, I went into the library and asked for a book on how to use my brain. The librarian pointed me to the medical section. When I explained that I did not wish to either operate on my brain or take it out but to *use* it, she gently explained that there were no such books on the topic.

From that day on my goal has been to investigate, learn, and teach information concerning the remarkable bio-computer that exists in all our heads, and to work with people who are not only similarly interested, but particularly capable of acquiring and imparting that information.

Fifteen years ago I had the privilege of meeting Kathryn Redway, who as you will increasingly realise from both this Foreword and this book, is one of those who is helping to fulfil my life's dream.

Kathryn is becoming increasingly known in the academic and professional fields for the lucid, witty and accessible way in which she presents up-to-date information on reading, learning, self-management, and generally keeping up with the information revolution.

Parallel with this development, is her increasing fame as an author of similar excellence.

In *Beat the Bumph!*, you too will have the privilege of conversing with her entertaining and scintillating mind. The book is packed with information, and is one of those rare volumes which delivers what it promises: a series of easily assimilatable formulas for accelerating all aspects of your interface with both printed and electronic data.

As the 21st century approaches, the most valuable asset of any individual, company or country is going to be its Intellectual Capital. The prime literacy is no longer going to be simply verbal or numerical, but Mental Literacy – the ability to understand the hardware and the software of our brains. The most powerful currency is not the yen, the Swiss franc, the German mark or the American dollar, but the currency of Intelligence.

Beat the Bumph! is a charming and delightful work that guarantees to make you instantaneously more Mentally Literate, and that should be a necessary addition to the book shelf of any individual learner or learning organisation interested in investing in their Intellectual Capital.

Contents

List of Figures   9
List of Tables   10
Preface   11

And thanking those who were involved in writing this
book...

INTRODUCTION

- Meet ... Bel and Ben Bumph, our fall-girl and guy,
  the twins, who get into all sorts of bumph problems
  in their offices and lives in general   12
- Learn ... the difference between information and
  bumph   13
- Decide ... how YOU will use this book to overcome
  your bumph problems   14

PART 1. DEFENCE AGAINST BUMPH   17

1   CONTROLLING BUMPH AND YOUR READING   18

- Adjust your attitude to tackle and beat bumph   19
- When you read you use visual and non-visual skills.
  Which do you need to brush up?   19
- We define understanding   21
- Reading and goals: What are you looking for?   22
- Define your goal and determine your reading
  strategy   25
- Use the power of anticipation and boost your
  confidence   26

2   CONTROLLING BUMPH AND YOUR TIME   28

- Do you suffer from piles?   29
- Brush up your delegation skills   29
- Make meetings less onerous and more effective   30
- Bel makes the transition from paperwork to information technology and the 'paperless' office   33
- Working with computers is easy if Bel regards them as high-speed idiots – lots of speed but not much sense if mismanaged   38

3   BINNING YOUR BUMPH   41

- Ever had too much unsolicited mail? Bin it!   42
- Are you a compulsive information collector? Weed it!   42
- The magazine is full of useless information? Gut it!   44

4   BEATING YOUR BUMPH BLOCKAGES   46

- Procrastination and interruptions. Do you, like Bel, put off necessary reading? Do you know how to discourage disrupting visitors and other inviting distractions?   47
- Memory. 'I remember the good old days because there were so few of them.' Do you want to remember more in the future? Here's how   49
- Recall. Follow your own pathways so that you can retrace them   55

PART 2. OFFENCE AGAINST BUMPH   57

5   BEAT THE BUMPH   58

- Ben Bumph is now ready to conquer infectious
  information. What prompts Ben into action? An
  awareness that there must be a better way   59
- Start with a log which records all the information
  you come across   61
- Analyse the pattern which emerges   62
- Do you ever think of the recipient when you send
  information?   62
- How instructive is the information you disseminate?
  Does the information help the recipient?   63

6   IMPROVE YOUR READING   67

- Myths that surround reading   68
- Do you know your reading speed? A simple exercise
  to determine your current speed   70
- Check Comprehension   74
- Subvocalisation. Do you always hear the words in
  your head when you read? This slows you down,
  but you can reduce and even eliminate this bad habit   75
- Concentration. To improve it, think of your physical
  surroundings as well as learn some simple steps to
  improve it   76
- Dyslexia, to a limited extent, affects many. Some
  methods to reduce its effects   79

7   IMPROVE YOUR VISUAL SKILLS   82

- Six exercises for collecting visual information
  effectively, with the emphasis on improving your
  reading speed:
  - Using motivation   85
  - Overcoming regression   86
  - Exploiting peripheral vision   88
  - Using a guide   91
  - Conditioning   94

Consolidating your gains 97
● Then learn to rest your eyes 98

8   SIX STEPS TO SYSTEMATIC READING 102

● The supreme test for Bel to absorb more in less time
and when to recognise bumph at a glance and reject
it 102
● Six steps for increasing your comprehension,
particularly with difficult, technical or uninviting
documents:
Recap: Brushing up your mind 104
Objectives: Set a goal before you start 104
Overview: Scan, get acquainted with the whole
document 106
Preview: Skim, reject the irrelevant or what you
know already 107
Inview: In-depth reading of new material 108
Review: Make a Mind Map® 109

9   APPLYING THE SIX STEPS TO READING ARTICLES 114

● Bel applies her newly learned skill to magazines and
newspapers:
The Financial Times 115
The Economist 118

10   HOW TO PRESENT AND EDIT A DOCUMENT 122

● Are you influenced by the presentation of a
document? So is everybody else. If you want to be
read your document must appear attractive:
Presentation examples 123
Eleven tips for attractive presentations 129
Four steps to edit a document 131

Bumph-free future ... 135
Bibliography 136
Index 137

List of Figures

1.1	A clock	22
1.2	A menu	23
1.3	A map	24
1.4	A bottle label	25
2.1	Examples of typefaces and sizes available	36
3.1	Advertising bumph in magazines	45
4.1	A model of the brain and memory	50
4.2	The principle behind mnemonics	52
4.3	How retention and recall ability decays	54
4.4	The basic Mind Map®	55
7.1	Untrained eye movements	87
7.2	Peripheral vision assessment	89
7.3	Eye movements using peripheral vision	90
7.4	Unguided eye movements	92
7.5	Guided eye movements	92
7.6	Using a finger as a reading guide or pacer	93
7.7	Fast reading conditioning with rhythm	95
8.1	What pattern fits this picture?	103
8.2	Mind Map®: *Pickwick Papers*	110
9.1	A *Financial Times* article	116
9.2	Mind Map® for *FT* article on Airbus	118
9.3	Article from *The Economist*	119
9.4	Mind Map® for article on optional investing	120
10.1	A typical book passage	124
10.2	Stock Market report, *The Times*, until mid 1993	125
10.3	How *The Times* improved the Stock Market report	126
10.4	Restyled book page	127
10.5	First impressions count	130
10.6	Four steps to edit a document	132

List of tables

2.1	A comparison of Bel's brain and the computer	38
5.1	Bumph log example	60
5.2	Bumph log	61
7.1	Results of reading exercises	84

Preface

Information and its evil twin brother 'bumph' are found on the airwaves, in boardrooms, in the classroom, in personal mail and in after-dinner speeches. New technology has spurred massive growth in the availability of information. This book aims to educate readers in how to meet these new challenges by adopting techniques that they never would have had the opportunity of picking up at school or college.

My initial thoughts on handling information were crystallised by Tony Buzan, to whom I am forever grateful. This book is intended to complement Tony's work, in particular the Brain Trust which he has founded. (The Use Your Head Club, PO Box 1821, Marlow, Bucks SL7 2YW, UK and The Buzan Centres, 37 Waterloo Road, Bournemouth, Dorset BH9 1BD, UK).

In writing this book I would like to thank all participants on my workshops who have contributed to updating my thinking, in particular Ken Baron of Bristol University who has sparked off interesting parallels between computer and mind; those members of IBM who started me thinking about reading on a VDU and writing into an electronic mail system. Thanks also go to Warner Books who have allowed me to use one of their books as an example (*A Whack on the Side of the Head*), and my publisher, Nicholas Brealey, whose judicious and imaginative comments tinted with a good sense of humour have made the job enjoyable.

I am also grateful to *The Economist, Financial Times* and *The Times* for permission to reproduce some of their material in Chapters 9 and 10.

Introduction

BEL AND BEN BUMPH – A CAUTIONARY TALE

Throughout this book the twins, Bel and Ben, will be our
bumph victims. As information management novices they are
thoroughly ill-equipped to face the barrage of material that
confronts them in their lives and jobs every day. But armed
with their trusty copies of *Beat the Bumph* they soon begin to
battle their way to well-managed lives and workloads. We
begin with a typical day for our flawed heroine, Bel.

> *Bel arrives at her office one morning, unpacks her briefcase and
> takes out a brown file, three magazines and half a dozen one-
> page memos. She also has a report which needs editing.*
>
> *In her 'out-tray' Bel places a magazine and all the one-page
> memos. Everything else stays on Bel's desk, joining yesterday's
> unfinished business in one large pile. She sighs as the post
> arrives on her desk: the stack is over an inch thick.*
>
> *Bel logs on to her computer and finds she has a dozen
> e-mail messages. Before retrieving them she glances at her
> diary and realises that she has only five minutes before she is
> due at an important meeting. She grabs her brown file as she
> hurries out of the door.*
>
> *As she slides into the meeting, a director is discussing
> whether a supplier should be changed. Bel struggles to
> remember the problem. Although she read the report late the
> night before she can only remember the name of the murderer
> in the film that was competing for her attention. To make up
> for her lapse of memory Bel makes copious notes, not knowing
> what information was in the report or even which issues are
> really relevant.*

> *When Bel returns to her office she attempts to tackle her e-mail and post, but a constant stream of interruptions and visitors prevents her from getting to grips with it. A lot of the stuff in her in-tray requires information which is not readily available — she puts these things aside. As she works, urgent faxes and calls distract her attention.*
>
> *As the day ends Bel fills up her briefcase, knowing that she will look at only a fraction of the material during the course of the evening. The report which needs editing also goes in. Despite trying to tackle it a few times she has not started it yet; even the appearance of the report seems to deter her.*

Our heroine, Bel, is being overwhelmed by information. Everything that comes across her desk seems useful and empowering yet, when facing the stream of facts, Bel is numb, unreceptive and unable to distinguish between valuable and unimportant information. She fails to return all her messages and many of her replies are past the deadlines required. Bel is suffering from infectious information. She needs to prepare offensive and defensive strategies.

In preparing a defensive strategy Bel needs to divide her material into information and bumph.

WHAT IS THE DIFFERENCE BETWEEN BUMPH AND INFORMATION?

'Bumph' (or bumf) — the piles of paperwork, reading matter and information that have to be dealt with but are of little interest, and that hinder you from accomplishing your primary tasks.

Bumph comes from the phrase 'bum fodder', meaning toilet paper. As you stare at the volumes of paper that crowd your desk, this might be worth remembering to set you in the right mental mood for discarding less useful material.

For our purposes the definition should be widened to include all the sources from which information is obtained. Bumph can obscure useful information in meetings, on the radio, in conversations, on the TV, as well as through all sorts of electronic media. All this information enters the brain and competes for attention, time and memory space as it is categorised, pigeon-holed, recalled and used at appropriate times.

Bumph may be likened to the snowstorm which obscures or hides the glimmer of light (information) towards which one is struggling. One of the aims of this book is to raise a fundamental issue: *As an information receiver, how frequently is the information you receive 'instructive'?* With a bit of practice you should find that extracting the useful from the bumph becomes an essential part of your routine and you will probably wonder how you ever coped before.

BEAT THE BUMPH AND YOU

This book is not designed to be read from cover to cover. Managing your time and information load should mean managing this book as well. If you are snowed under like Bel Bumph then the last thing you need is a lot of extra reading. The chapters of this book are designed to be used as units. You can read straight through or skip from chapter to chapter. At the end of each chapter, start off on the technique that you have just learned using the exercises.

Now I am making a foolish assumption: you have some problems with information flow and you want an easier life. Do some of these general problems apply to you?

- You receive many documents and your e-mail is cluttered up with many types of information which will never be of interest to you.
- You receive information of little or no use to you.
- You spend too long in meetings or reading information.
- You have difficulty in assessing clearly the purpose for which you need the information contained in a particular document (or information source).
- Few meetings or documents are crucial or very important to you for the effective performance of your job.

- In a particular document the information you want is highly diluted by information you do not want.
- You feel guilty about the piles of manuals, periodicals and reports waiting to be read.
- You think other people manage their 'bumph' but you don't.
- You are unsure about what information to keep and how to file it.
- You have discovered that taking decisions, generally, is a painful process.

Specifically, in handling bumph, do you recognise any of the following difficulties?

	Go to Chapter
- Felt that a document was uninviting and left it aside?	6
- Re-read a word, a paragraph, a page, for fear of missing something?	6
- Had difficulty in finding your way around a document?	8
- Found it difficult to make notes from a document?	8
- Invested much time to absorb and retain information and then forgotten it?	4
- Wondered which document to tackle first?	2
- Experienced poor concentration?	6
- Felt you had to remember everything you read?	6
- Wished you could extract 'important' information fast?	8
- Found that you did not understand what you read?	8

With meetings, these are the most commonly cited problems. Have you ever:

- Felt that you attended too many meetings?
- Been to meetings which were badly chaired?
- Had difficulty writing the agenda or the minutes?
- Felt the topics discussed in meetings overlapped?
- Wished meetings ended on time?

Go to Chapter 2

Part 1
Defence against Bumph

Chapter 1
Controlling Bumph and Your Reading

- **READING IS AN ATTITUDE**
- **VISUAL AND NON-VISUAL SKILLS**
- **READING AND UNDERSTANDING**
- **SO, WHAT HAVE WE LEARNED?**
- **READING AND GOALS**
- **THE POWER OF ANTICIPATION IN READING**
- **HANDS-ON EXERCISES**

READING IS AN ATTITUDE

Technology has freed our hero Ben from many boring and
tedious tasks. It has, however, resulted in a massive increase in
the amount of information capable of changing hands. In a
week Ben comes across more information than the average
person in 19th century Europe received in a year.

Today information is mass produced, controlled and driven
by your expectations. How many unsolicited offers or letters
have you received this week? What information did your
organisation or boss restrict? What information do you hear a
great deal on English television that never appears on German
television? How frequently do you hear without listening? See
without perceiving? Read without understanding?

Handling this massive influx of bumph requires the right
mental attitude. To face the problems head on you and Ben
need:

★ *the desire to improve.* You have to be prepared to increase
  your reading speed, your time management and your ability
  to identify essential information. Opening this book is an
  important first step.

★ *confidence.* It is important to improve and believe that you
  can.

★ *assertiveness.* You must accept that you do not need to know
  everything by recognising that some information is
  irrelevant while other bits of information are vital for you.

★ *the ability to relax.* Once rid of anxiety you will find it easier
  to use memory, organise information, rely on your current
  knowledge, and establish your reading objectives.

**To control bumph be: motivated, confident, assertive,
relaxed.**

VISUAL AND NON-VISUAL SKILLS

When you read a phrase your brain dissects it in a number of
different ways. It is capable of recognising whole words and
phrases in hundredths of a second without the need to

consider each letter. To demonstrate this consider the following passage:

Es war Anfang Mai und, nach nasskalten wochen, ein falscher Hochsommer eingefallen. Der Englische Garten, obgleich nur erst zart belaubt, war dumpfig wie im August und in der Nähe, der Stadt voller Wagen und Spaziergänger gewesen.

(from *Der Tod in Venedig* by Thomas Mann)

If you are unable to speak German, the only way you can read it is by examining each word and guessing how it might be pronounced. As only one or two of the words have any obvious meaning this is quite a slow process. You will find your eye often needs to examine each word a few times. Compare this to something in English where recognition can be used:

A wonderful bird is the pelican,
His bill will hold more than his belican.
He can take in his beak
Food enough for a week,
But I'm damned if I see how the helican.

(D. L. Merritt, 1879–1954)

The words in this limerick are familiar and some even evoke images so they are instantly recognised by the brain. You probably found that you had more difficulty with the last word in the last line and the last word in the second line. Your brain was unable to recognise the 'shape' of these words so it had to hover over them a little longer to examine each letter.

This process is the same for whole phrases. Try reading what you see below quite quickly:

Paris
in the
the spring

Unless you are a very slow and careful reader you will have thought that the phrase said 'Paris in the spring'. Look again and you will see that it actually says 'Paris in *the the* spring'. Your brain is adept at recognising whole phrases which are familiar in very small periods of time. This enables you to scan very quickly through documents looking for information if you discipline your mind in the right way.

READING AND UNDERSTANDING

It is also important to remember that your brain connects whole sentences to other sentences and can relate this to other information from the rest of your knowledge base. To illustrate this, consider the following:

But silver bromide is so much less soluble than silver chloride that a far smaller concentration of potassium bromide will produce a precipitate, while silver iodide, the least soluble of the three, is precipitated in very low iodide concentrations. This method can be used to separate silver chloride from silver iodide. The usual explanation is that 'silver chloride is more soluble in ammonia than silver iodide' but this is not a satisfactory way of stating the facts.
(from *Theoretical and Inorganic Chemistry*, Philbrick and Holmyard, p 190).

Unless you are well versed in the solubility of silver halides in ammonia solutions, the chances are that you cannot remember the information in the passage. If you do remember, it is unlikely that you will remember it half an hour from now. So your ability to retain information is very dependent upon your understanding of and familiarity with the subject matter.

To summarise, good understanding involves:

★ Being able to select and understand what you need
★ Connecting this new information to existing knowledge
★ Retaining and recalling that information

SO, WHAT HAVE WE LEARNED?

When you read, your brain is involved in the following simultaneous steps:

• Visual recognition of symbols: words which are not familiar are read by examining each character.
• Visual recognition of whole words or phrases: whole-word recognition is facilitated by its position in a logical phrase.
• Comprehension and the integration into semantic – or related – knowledge: a process of evaluating the knowledge.

- Memorising the information.
- Responding to the information: what do you do with it?

Visual and non-visual skills can be improved. The simple task of improving visual skills is described in Chapter 7. We call it improving the dynamics of reading. It is easy.

Much more challenging are the non-visual components of reading: using imagery, increasing comprehension, and improving long-term retention of information. These are dealt with in Chapters 4, 6 and 8.

READING AND GOALS

To obtain information quickly when reading it is important to have a goal. You adopt different reading strategies depending upon the type of information you want to extract.

Imagine you are reading the time on a clock. If you wish to catch a train, the clock tells you how long you have to do this in comfort. The *goal of reading the clock* in this context is to calculate the time you have left to catch the train.

Figure 1.1 A clock

How did you read the menu last time you were in a restaurant? If you are vegetarian, you will have skipped the meat dishes. If you were on a budget you only considered dishes in your price range. The *goal of reading the menu* is a selective process in which large sections of the menu are discarded before a dish is chosen.

Menu

Hors d'Oeuvres

Mousse aux Courgettes 1.50
Coulis de Poivrons doux et Tomates 2.50
Provençal Hors d'Oeuvres 2.50
Onions à la Greque 2.00

Vegetarian

Avacado Pilaff 6.00
Watercress Salad with Mushrooms 5.50
Walnut Roll 5.50
Fettuccine al Burro e Formaggio 7.50

Fish

Salmon Croquettes 9.00
Bouillabaisse Salad 9.50
Devilled Whitebait 8.00
Crab Salad 9.50

Entrées

Agneau Epicé 10.00
Boeuf en Daube 8.95
Osso Bucco 10.50
Steak and Kidney Pudding 10.50

Poultry

Pheasant with Lentils 10.50
Timbale of Duck 9.00
Roast Chicken with Watercress Stuffing 8.50
Braised Ortolans 11.50

Desserts

Lemon Sorbet 1.30
Cassatta alla Siciliana 1.50
Normandy Baked Apples 1.50
Strawberries with Marsala and Pernod 2.10

Café 1.50

Figure 1.2 A menu

If you are reading a map you will probably want to know how to get to your destination and how long it will take you. The *goal of reading a map* is to find out which roads lead from one place to another and to plan your route.

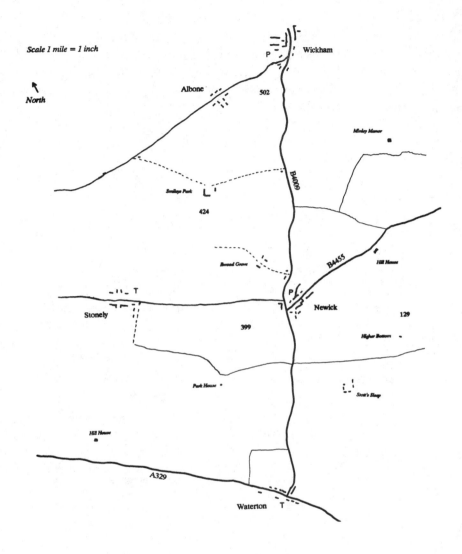

Figure 1.3 A map

If you have a family member who is allergic to some food then you have to scan product labels to find the offending ingredient. In my family I have to read food labels to see if the product contains monosodium glutamate. The *goal of reading the label* is to ascertain whether the product is 'safe'.

When opened consume at once.

Spooner's Somerset Sauce

**The perfect compliment to alcoholic
and night-time beverages**
By appointment to his late majesty King
George IV

"Never again will I touch a good malt whiskey
without lacing it with a few drops of SSS."
General G.S. (Ret'd) of Cheltenham.
"Every night I sleep like a log since I started
to make my Hollicks with SSS." Granny G. of
Princeton.

Made to a unique secret recipe by S.
Spooner and Company since 1793

INGREDIENTS:- MATURED BOMBAY DUCK, OLD MOLASSES,
DEHYDRATED EGGS, DRIED SNOEK, FRUCTOSE, MONOSO-
DIUM GLUTAMATE, EMULSIFIERS E471, E472, E475, COL-
OURS (LUTEIN, BETA-CAROTENE, RIBOFLAVIN),
LACTOALBUMEN, STABILISER (CARRAGEENAN).

Figure 1.4 A bottle label

These examples show that visual information is not enough
to achieve the goal of the reading exercise. We use different
reading strategies depending on the goal. You read telephone
directories, newspapers, and instructions to install a video-
recorder in different ways. You read with a purpose in mind
which interacts with the information you are reading and the
knowledge you already have. If you neglect to think about
purpose or goals first, you are likely to choose the wrong
reading strategy.

THE POWER OF ANTICIPATION IN READING

Have you ever tried to read a complex legal document? Unless you are a lawyer you will probably find you have to read every word of a contract in order to understand it. Lack of familiarity with the subject and with the words used make it difficult for you to guess or anticipate what you are going to read.

Try picking up a newspaper and selecting an article. Can you make sense of it by reading only half the printed words? Try to eliminate or abandon roughly five words per sentence. If you are familiar with the style and subject matter then you will find this task a lot easier.

Imagine that you are half-way through a thriller. The action takes place in a European city in the middle of summer. When you pick up the book again, will you be thinking 'The author hasn't mentioned penguins yet. I wonder if he'll describe the breeding condition of penguins on the shores of the Antarctic?' Probably not. Instead you may be anticipating likely thrilling events taking place in the summer in Europe.

Similarly a sentence which begins 'Management books are written around themes, reports contain specific information and minutes of meetings' is not likely to be followed by *eat, elephant, trumpet* or *rhododendron*. You can make a reasonable guess, amongst 100,000 alternatives. The possible words are selected because the context limits choice. *Develop and use your power of anticipation*. Have the confidence of previous experience, previous knowledge and familiarity with the context which will enable your mind to speed up your comprehension of the text.

Dr Bates, an American ophthalmologist, in *Better Eyesight Without Glasses* (10), wrote 'We see very largely with the mind, and only partly with the eyes'. To paraphrase his belief it can be argued that we read largely with the mind and only partly with the eyes.

HANDS-ON EXERCISES

☛ Keep a record of all non-work related reading material that you receive and make a note of its purpose.

☛ Develop anticipation by reading one paragraph of a document upside-down.

☛ Practise picking an article in a newspaper and deliberately reading only one word in three. Summarise the article. Are you missing much of importance?

Chapter 2
Controlling Bumph and Your Time

DO YOU SUFFER FROM PILES?

DELEGATING

MINIMISING MEETING TIME

DEALING WITH ELECTRONIC TEXT

ERADICATE COMPUTER BUMPH

HANDS-ON EXERCISES

DO YOU SUFFER FROM PILES?

Like Bel, most people suffer from 'priority piles'. Which pile of untouched work deserves priority? Different demands on time require prioritising.

All work can be categorised as:

- urgent, must be attended to immediately,
- should be completed within the next few days,
- can be put aside (if other things are pressing) for a week or so, or
- need never do.

There is a fifth category: the sort of job where you can save a lot of time and stress by doing parts of it as you come across it in the course of current or urgent work. For example, you have to give a presentation in four weeks' time. Rather than waiting for the job to move into the urgent category you can gradually assemble the information required whenever you come across appropriate data. Collecting the data, unedited and unsorted in a file awaiting attention, saves much hassle in the days immediately before its delivery. Otherwise, as Murphy's Law forecasts, if you start looking for the information only at the last moment, it will not be available and a crisis will develop.

While you should give your full attention to one task at a time, you should group your work load into two piles:

★ The first pile contains jobs which require immediate attention and action.

★ The second pile contains documents which require some time to be read or which can only be dealt with after more information has been assembled.

DELEGATING

Bel should never forget the concept of delegation. Always she should try to identify the work, perhaps part of a task for which she is responsible, that could be done by somebody else and then delegate it.

Work can be delegated in three directions:

- It can be delegated *upwards* if your boss does not give you full authority to complete a task. It stands to reason that if you are unable to finish something without help from above then you can request help to do your work.
- Delegation *sideways* comes about by having a colleague who is better equipped to do a job than you are. This usually happens if they have specialist knowledge, control the resources or are not under the same time constraints as you.
- Delegation *downwards* is the most obvious. Junior staff quite often appreciate this because it shows your trust in them or it enables them to develop skills that they might eventually market elsewhere.

MINIMISING MEETING TIME

Bel finds that one of her most frequent bumph problems is associated with meetings that are poorly chaired, occur too frequently or go on for too long.

MINIMISE THE FREQUENCY, MAXIMISE THE EFFICIENCY

Meetings can be too frequent and often topics overlap. It is always worth exploring the alternatives:

- ★ How about circulating widely a memo for people to approve or comment? E-mail makes this very efficient. Two drawbacks are that often one does not get the benefit of interaction or the synthesis of ideas.
- ★ Conference calls or video links can save a lot of travelling time but can be quite difficult to chair if there are too many people.
- ★ It is always worth attempting to amalgamate meetings. Could 'one hour, monthly' meetings replace '45 minutes, fortnightly'?

★ If meetings are essential to decision making, remember that with more than four people coming to a conclusion becomes much more difficult.

★ Rather than attending meetings ask instead for a copy of the minutes.

★ What are the risks of *not* attending some meetings?

★ Develop the habit of saying 'No' if you cannot see how attending a meeting can contribute anything or be useful to you.

SHORTEN THE LENGTH OF MEETINGS

Frequently short meetings are the most effective. If you are arranging a meeting do you always take the following steps?

★ Prepare a detailed agenda. For example, instead of 'Computer system installation schedule', write: 'Computer system installation is four weeks behind schedule and £6,000 overrun caused by supplier difficulties. The meeting is to consider how the installation can get back onto schedule and within budget, how supplier difficulties can be reduced and what action can be taken to minimise current problems'. List who is to contribute what.

★ Estimate the timetable for decision(s) to be made during the meeting and list it on the agenda.

★ Choose a finishing time that will create a sense of urgency, for example just before lunch or, best of all, on a Friday afternoon.

★ Put less important items at the front of the agenda to minimise latecomers' disorientation, with important items in the middle and a popular, easily agreed item last, to end the meeting on an up-beat note of achievement.

★ Ensure that all attendees are properly briefed about difficult or complex subjects beforehand to eliminate time wastage in the meeting.

★ Suggest holding the meeting in someone else's office. It is easier to leave a colleague's office than one's own.

Here is a checklist you can use as a reminder:

Improve Your Management of Meetings

✓ *Before the Meeting*

✓ 1. Ensure that a programme or agenda is prepared. Outline the purpose of the meeting clearly. The agenda also states the beginning and finishing time, date, place and names of participants.

✓ 2. Notify all appropriate people to attend. Supply agenda and necessary briefing papers, allow time enough for them to be read in advance.

✓ 3. Book a room for the meeting with appropriate facilities.

✓ 4. Nominate a secretary or scribe, making sure he or she knows their duties. If possible, have overhead projector (OHP) transparencies or flipcharts prepared beforehand.

✓ 5. Check that all invitees can attend.

✓ *During the Meeting*

✓ 6. Start on time, even if people are missing.

✓ 7. The chairperson:
  - ✓ reiterates the purpose of the meeting
  - ✓ defines the facts and constraints of the situation
  - ✓ establishes the task(s) of the meeting

✓ 8. The chairperson guides people through the meeting. He or she ensures that the subject of the meeting is adhered to, formulates questions to act as a catalyst and develops group interest and involvement.

✓ 9. All members should participate. If not, why?

✓10. The scribe keeps notes and uses an OHP or flipchart to display key concepts, suggestions, parameters, etc.

✓11. Recap progress regularly, points of agreement and disagreement. Check understanding and acceptance.

✓12. Acknowledge all contributions, including those not used. Recognise degrees of feeling and changes of opinion.

✓13. Allow limited excursions from the subject if they appear to be opening up an important new line of thought which may affect the subject. Suggest, if appropriate, that these be made the subject of action after the meeting and perhaps the subject of a subsequent meeting.

✓14. Delegate action items and unresolved issues to attendees for action outside the meeting, so that problems are answered without the need for another meeting, or proper preparation is made for the next meeting.

✓15. Obtain agreement on responsibility for action and deadlines.

✓16. Maintain a spirit of enthusiasm and good humour.

✓17. Finish firmly on time.

✓*After the meeting*

✓18. Ensure that accurate minutes are issued and distributed to all attendees within two days, with decisions and future actions, by whom and when clearly noted.

✓19. The minutes can be circulated to those persons who need to be informed of decisions made in the meeting but did not attend.

DEALING WITH ELECTRONIC TEXT

Techniques for dealing with computer text do not differ radically from techniques for dealing with other types of bumph. It is therefore a little surprising that people expect a brand new technique to cope with electronic mail or other electronically driven documents! Bel could apply the same basic instructions that she uses for paper to a screen.

Ten Easy Steps to Reading a Screen

✓ To read faster, use the scroll mechanism or the cursor (or caret) as a pacer or prompter.
✓ Set time limits when the text is longer than two pages.
✓ Avoid printing out the message, even if it is two or three pages long.
✓ Use the techniques of scanning and skimming to pick up keywords to decide whether messages are worth reading thoroughly.
✓ Check your messages regularly – say a minimum of twice a day – so as to avoid electronic 'piles'. In some organisations messages are automatically erased after a few hours if individuals have not checked them: the idea is to prompt people into a discipline, and it works! If you are away from your office, log in regularly.
✓ Avoid glare. Tilt the screen at an angle so that the bottom is lifted slightly towards you.
✓ Avoid working in the dark with only the screen as a source of light.
✓ Rest your eyes by doing some exercises. Close your eyes for a full minute and imagine the colour black. Put the palm of your hands over your eyes to help see darkness. Or go to a window and stare at one point far in the distance for five seconds, and then without moving your head stare for five seconds at the nearest point to you. Repeat every 20 minutes or so.
✓ Schedule your day to take breaks at least every hour to relax the body. Do other tasks, for example make a telephone call or go to see somebody.
✓ Sit on an adaptable chair that will support the small of your back.

As for reading on paper, a lot of problems occur on a monitor screen because the writer did not think of the reader's needs. The way the message is conveyed must not obscure the message. The format of the message should enhance it. So here are a few tips to write better, electronically.

Ten Easy Steps to Writing on a Screen

✓ Do you need to write this note? Would a phone call or a meeting be more efficient?

✓ Keep your memos short. One screen length, if you can. Memos are not designed to debate facts; they are designed to convey facts.

✓ Simplify. Keep the message simple and to the point. Do not use the traditional long heading used for written memos.

✓ Consistency is essential in preparation and use of words.

✓ Use different fonts and point sizes to emphasise the important part of your message. Bold type is effective but less readable. Italics are subtle and more readable. Avoid underlining. An example of the kind of fonts available in most systems is given in Figure 2.1.

✓ If you are writing a short message, capitals are the equivalent of shouting at someone.

✓ Use symbols and indentations. Hanging indents give good paragraph separation but add to length.

✓ Leave gaps between paragraphs.

✓ Do not send your message to people who do not need it.

✓ Apply the twice-a-year rule: tidy up your files twice a year, eliminating about 70%. Disk storage is expensive.

But of course there is more to using technology than brushing up one's skills or technique. With the advance of communications via computer, the nature of one's work is radically changed. Two areas are affected: one is loss of individuality, the other is a reinforced centralisation.

When, in the past, oral or written communications were used, it was easy to identify the author of the instructions. Today, an electronic text may be the sum of several individual acts. For example, monthly sales figures will be produced by the inputs of several different functions or branches collected together to make one piece of information. Individuality has to give way to conformity to local standards.

This typeface may be called Helvetica Bold,

or BOLD ITALICS

This typeface may be called Engravers Old English, (but it isn't).

How about some GOTHIC?

This typeface may be

Sans Serif italic.

Here we have Times, Baskerville, Bodoni or Roman bold, the classic,

and it may range in size from this to

THIS LARGE SIZE.

What do you think OF THIS TYPEFACE?

Figure 2.1 Examples of Typefaces and Sizes Available

To convey information electronically, an organisation collects a wide range of data and codifies this information in a single computer system. At first, this seems cold, remote and noiseless. The effort an individual puts into gathering and conveying information produces different results. Authorship is lost but the number of people able to read it has increased enormously.

Bumph, Culture and Information Technology

A blue-chip multinational was about to move from scattered offices to a prestigious, centralised building. Part of the policy behind the move was to introduce information technology in each department. Until then, it had been a haphazard affair. Each employee was to have a micro-processor and was meant to use it. Before the move, courses were organised to allow those who needed to to catch up with typing skills, computer literacy and so on. A week after the move was completed, the Managing Director called in his most senior colleagues and demonstrated how to use the machine. He then exhorted his colleagues to pass the message on down the line. They did so. Within two months two thousand staff had abandoned the old way of doing things. All were using their newly installed technology.

For the visitor, this presented an extraordinary contrast. One arrived on a floor and the most striking feature was the silence. Office doors were open, but no one seemed to talk. People were sitting at keyboards, peering at screens. Telephone usage was halved, meetings reduced in number: people used the electronic mail system. And yet, human contact had been preserved. A large café area had been installed, complete with waitress service. Staff could sit down or, continental style, stand at the bar. The noise in there was phenomenal. People were having face-to-face exchanges over a hot chocolate or an expresso. The office had become an efficient, silent working place. The paperless bumph happened in the café!

Bel is often bemused by the jargon used by her IT colleagues. But many of the methods a computer uses to work are similar to what goes on in our brains: there are input recognition, processing, sorting, short- and long-term memory, and recall systems, just as Bel has.

You can use this comparison to work out how to get the computer to help you solve a problem, for instance how to distribute selected information to certain people, or assemble and manipulate data for a report. Also, when talking to computer experts or information systems support staff, you can translate their jargon into normal words and use everyday analogies to describe what you want. The sensible IT expert has no excuse for confusing you with techno-babble or bumph. Table 2.1 highlights some of the similarities and correspondences between our brains and computers, while doing the same job – processing information. So you can talk to your computer as you can to a human being!

Table 2.1   A Comparison of Bel's Brain and the Computer

COMPUTER MEMORY	HUMAN MEMORY
Processor memory – fast	Short-term memory (STM) – fast
Disk or tape memory – slow	Long-term memory – slow
Hierarchical or relational, data can be stored according to use frequency or data relationships	Short- or long-term memory depends on frequency of use and emotional (relational) impact
Cache memory holds recently accessed data	Short-term memory
Object orientation (reducing complex, different input to a common base)	Memory links data to images, sounds, smells

COMPUTER INPUT/ OUTPUT	BRAIN INFORMATION INPUT/OUTPUT
Reactive input via keyboard, touch screen, mouse	Input by sight, sound, smell, touch and taste
Output by printer, speech synthesiser, VDU screen	Output by writing, talking, movement
Data input via tape, disk, network	Knowledge input via book, video, talk

COMPUTER PROCESSING	BRAIN PROCESSING
Process by using software instructions to sort, store, compare	Process by sorting (recognition), store in STM, use rules (comparison)
Coprocessor specialises in high-speed mathematical calculations	Specialist operations, e.g. recalling telephone directory

COMPUTER AND READING	HUMAN RAPID READING
Clock speed	Reading rhythm
Byte, an 8 bit representation of character	A letter, numeral, space or punctuation mark
Fixed field length	A letter, numeral, space or punctuation mark
Record	Word
File, a logical collection of data	Book, or a structured chapter
Random access via a pointer	Dipping randomly into a book
Fixed length record	Variable length word or number
Variable length record is unusual	Groups of words or phrases
Blocked records, one read operation shows several records	Peripheral vision views several words per line and several lines simultaneously

INCREASING COMPUTER SPEED	INCREASING READING SPEED
Increase clock speed	Increase reading rhythm
Increase size of memory	Nil
Use memory management	Train to use memory techniques
Add processors	Share the task with a friend
Use multi-tasking	Concentrate on scanning, processing and output are handled by the subconscious
Data transfer by large block size	Increase scanned blocks with peripheral vision
Data caching, high speed buffer	Expand short-term memory by practice
INCREASING COMPUTER ACCURACY	**INCREASING READING COMPREHENSION**
Re-reading	Re-reading
Parity bit and check digit	Nil
Checksum, of whole field	Check block sense
Change clock speed	Change rhythm to suit material difficulty/ familiarity

HANDS-ON EXERCISES

☞ If you have several piles of bumph, simplify them into two piles as described in this chapter. Discard the remainder *now!*

☞ Become more alert to the need to attend meetings. Could you drop out of a regular one? What would happen if you did not attend?

☞ Discuss with colleagues the presentation of documents via electronic mail. Can it be simplified?

☞ Explain how your computer works to a ten-year-old; do not lapse into jargon; use words and experiences the child understands!

Chapter 3
Binning your Bumph

UNSOLICITED MAIL FACTS

LIMIT YOUR INFORMATION COLLECTION

GUTTING MAGAZINES

HANDS-ON EXERCISES

UNSOLICITED MAIL FACTS

Ben was not surprised to learn that the average UK business person receives 14 items of direct mail each week (14). Of the 588 million items of business direct mail sent out by suppliers in 1992 about 2% generated business, but throwing away 61% of this vast amount consumed a significant amount of business time, especially as some of it was read before it was thrown away.

And the same story is developing on Ben's electronic mail system. How is he to cope with the bumph?

LIMIT YOUR INFORMATION COLLECTION

 A Cautionary Tale

During recessionary times the Sales Director of a company manufacturing concrete products for the construction industry had an idea. Why not enter another sector of the concrete product business, diversify, extend the product range into fancy garden paving, decorative tubs, concrete fencing and concrete garden furniture? The idea seemed great. A whole new market opened up in his mind.

The first morning back in the office he instructed some of his staff to find out all they could about concrete 'garden' products made for the retail market, garden centres, builders and do-it-yourself merchants. What sort of products were already on sale? What prices, designs, type of sales inducements? Within a few days diligent staff reappeared with an astonishingly large volume of brochures, pamphlets and price lists.

This rang an alarm bell in the Sales Director's head. He called the library enquiry desk of his trade association. Please could they let him have the trade breakdown figures for the 'domestic' or DIY sector of the concrete products business? A day or two later a few pages of information appeared on his desk. It showed that the market was saturated with manufacturers, with an enormous range of products and qualities. Competition was cut-throat in garden DIY products. And compared with the wholesale construction industry, the

> *DIY industry was a pygmy. Obviously it was not worth fighting for a segment of a small market, far better to put renewed effort into their main market, and try to find some innovative new products or marketing or quality improvement methods there.*

Collecting information without a clear objective works against more important information for which a clear requirement exists. All the information except the last two or three sheets collected by the Sales Director above was a waste of time. His first enquiry should have been to his trade association. The first question should have been 'What is the status of the garden products market?' before getting down to the nitty-gritty of what products there were and how much they cost.

The anecdote describes an attitude of mind which believes that to take decisions one needs to assemble as much information as possible. What is needed, in fact, is to gather only the *relevant* or *necessary* information. Here are four rules to avoid information overload:

★ **Ask yourself what type of information you really need.** Think in terms of *purpose*, not accumulation. Reading too much data can cloud a manager's judgement and slow down the decision-making process.

★ **Be critical** of raw statistics and measurements, like the typical 1.2 children per family in some countries, or the public opinion poll which indicates that 64.73% of people have a certain view, when only 1,000 people were questioned. Such accuracy may be useful for your purpose, but take significant effort to produce. Inaccuracy may be more common: either the methods of measurement are wrong, or an error has occurred or a set of figures ignores something that has changed. For example, there was a time when people believed that all cholesterol was bad. But what is important about cholesterol is the proportion of HDL (high density lipoprotein, 'good' cholesterol) to LDL (low density lipoprotein, 'bad' cholesterol).

★ **Network** or discuss with people who have specialist knowledge. They have already collected the data and can give you meaningful information.

★ **Keep a wide range of information sources open.** If you ask yourself 'What will I do with the information?' you will find that you will make links between a variety of items that you learn and many of those items you already know. A wide range of information sources encourages you to think and mull ideas around; thinking makes you better informed.

GUTTING MAGAZINES

Are you one of these people who uses commuting time to good effect by reading magazines and journals in the train or underground? Well done! But what about the time it takes you to find what you want among all those pages, and what about the weight of what you carry back and forth?

The proportion of advertising material to articles in magazines is surprising (see Figure 3.1). Some typical issues of magazines and journals contain the following amounts of advertising:

● A typical issue of *The Economist* – 42% of its pages
● *Chemistry in Britain* – 38% of its contents
● *The Director*, published by the Institute of Directors – 36%
● The Institute of Management journal *Management Today* – 42%

To reduce your article search time (and your luggage weight) tear the advertising bumph out of your magazines and keep the rest. But if you are interested in only one or two articles in the magazine after you have skimmed through the table of contents and flicked through the summary or first paragraph of all articles, tear those articles out of the magazine.

If you cannot tear up a magazine because it is a circulation copy or belongs to someone else, get someone to photocopy the articles you are interested in, and pass it on quickly to minimise the amount of bumph on your desk.

Figure 3.1 Advertising bumph in magazines

HANDS-ON EXERCISES

☛ Can you delegate sifting through unsolicited mail to an assistant? Decide that at present you are interested in training matters, but not in buying more books, or joining more clubs or institutes. Your bumph may be reduced by 70%.

☛ Stop people in meetings who go into unnecessary detail or throw in figures that are not relevant to the subject under discussion.

☛ Practice gutting your own personal magazines.

Chapter 4
Beating Your Bumph Blockages

REDUCING PROCASTINATION AND INTERRUPTIONS

IMPROVE MEMORY AND RECALL

USE RECALL PATTERNS

HANDS-ON EXERCISES

Our heroine, Bel Bumph, has reports to read and correct, a contract to study and several unpalatable decisions to take. But today is only Tuesday and she thinks 'I have the rest of the week to deal with them'. Wednesday goes by; Bel adds more to the list. Thursday arrives. Bel wants to begin the day tackling the list. But a voice in her head says 'Are you sure you won't get interrupted? Shouldn't you chase up yesterday's unfinished business first? What about making that phone call while you have the time? Besides, you have all of tomorrow.' 'That's quite true,' thinks Bel. 'I'll do it then.'

In the meantime, two of her subordinates are infuriated by her habit of postponing decisions. They complain bitterly behind her back: 'She has all the information she needs. Now is the time to take a decision but, once more, she'll wait until tomorrow and then ask us to provide unnecessary work.'

On Friday morning, Bel has to deal with an unforeseen crisis. It takes most of her time. By four o'clock Bel is tired and cross with herself. 'I just have no self-discipline; it is a vicious circle.' What a way to begin the weekend!

Bel is a procrastinator, enduring life rather than enjoying it, caught in the spiral of never having enough time to do things, or having enough information to take decisions. She does not set a specific time to achieve tasks. Without a written reminder our heroine excludes what she does not like from her schedule. Though it is difficult for someone like Bel to change her habits, there are many ways she can regain control of her life.

REDUCE PROCRASTINATION AND INTERRUPTIONS

Slow readers like Bel and those faced with an unpleasant reading task tend to put off reading as much as they can, for as long as they can. If you belong to this group you need to understand the reasons for your behaviour. It is because either:

- you perceive reading as an unpleasant, long, tiresome task, or

- the material is complex and overwhelming and you may not know how and where to start.

If the material is complex and overwhelming, it should help if you follow some of these rules:

★ **Start now**. Remember the Chinese proverb: 'A 1,000 mile march starts with the first step'. The 'now effect' reduces the gap between thought and action. Plunge right in; don't listen to inner voices that are tempting you away.

★ Divide the material into **chunks**. Concentrated 20 minute bits throughout the morning are better than spending a whole morning on something that should have taken one hour.

★ Give yourself **deadlines**. If you are researching for something, set a time to finish reading three of the papers, or chapters. If you receive reports, which day of the week will you circulate them, or send them to the central filing system? Enter your self-imposed deadlines in your diary or on your list of jobs for today, as you would with other appointments and engagements. Set definite starting and finishing times for particular reading tasks. Get a clock or timer and set it.

★ **Involve** a colleague if possible. Say you are researching this or that, or that you need to make a decision on this or that report and you would like their opinion when you have read it. Set a time for your work together.

★ **Congratulate** yourself as you are moving along. Consider what you have achieved and that it is not so complicated after all. (This is another reason why breaking the material into chunks is helpful.)

Preparation for serious reading means getting ready mentally. Beware of interruptions or, more insidiously, waiting or expecting to be distracted. Sometimes we create our own interruptions; often the greatest culprit is ourselves. Faced with an unpleasant task, how often have you given yourself the excuse of calling someone with no good reason, to deal with a low priority query, or just for a chat, and interrupting that person! Or have you ever been thinking 'there is no point in my starting this now, I am bound to be interrupted as soon as I start', and sure enough, you are and you rejoice! Interruptions can be controlled. To reduce their negative effects, here are some guidelines:

★ Don't be your own worst enemy: if you recognise yourself in the paragraph above, decide to do something about it, for example:

★ Tell others that you need to study a document and do not want to be disturbed.

★ If you have an 'open door' policy, shut it when you need time to yourself. One to two hours per day is reasonable.

★ Ask your secretary or a colleague to take phone calls and to discourage visitors for the time you need.

★ Find a quiet place or office for, say, one hour, and do not tell anyone where you are.

★ Come to the office early in the morning, before the phone starts ringing or people are in, one day a week. Alternatively, stay late one day a week. Early is best, because your mind and the day are fresh.

Dealing with obstinate visitors

If people ignore your message that you wish to be undisturbed, stand up when they approach your desk. Someone perceived to be on the move gives the message that he or she is in a hurry. Don't sit down. Ask how long their query will last. If more than five minutes, refuse to discuss it now. Say that your mind is on something else and that their problem requires your full attention. Make an appointment that is mutually convenient. Avoid eye contact from now on and firmly accompany the person out of the room.

IMPROVE MEMORY AND RECALL

You will recall how Bel was struggling to remember facts in a meeting. Like you, perhaps, she frequently blames her memory. Part of your defence to beat the bumph is to develop a better memory system. Imagine your memory as a filing cabinet with a couple of drawers containing the right amount of files, neatly ordered. Someone asks you a question: you open the appropriate drawer, pick up the correct file and provide the answer.

Unfortunately people's memory is not always so carefully organised. Someone asks a question: you open a drawer at random and find nothing relevant there, or the file is missing and you have a blank – literally!

To explain and remedy the problem we need to examine memory a little. *Memory consists of taking in information, storing it and retrieving it.* Psychologists further divide memory into working or short-term memory and long-term memory. Schematically, it looks like the model in Figure 4.1.

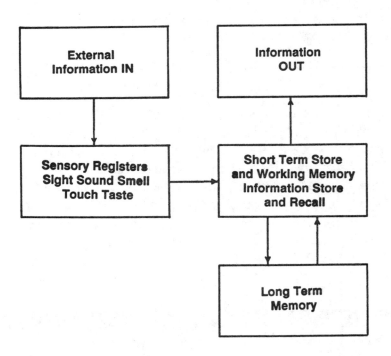

Figure 4.1 A Model of the Brain and Memory

GETTING INTERESTED

So, where do problems lie? First you must make sure that the information goes in, otherwise it certainly will not be retrieved! Do you frequently suffer from total memory loss after, say, one hour of learning something? This is probably a remnant of the school system which emphasises cramming information to pass exams at the expense of raising an interest in the subject. Before you take in information and, therefore, remember it, there must be interest. You need to stimulate your curiosity. Try to attune past experience to the new knowledge in front of you.

Some people confuse interest and obligations. Think of the things you do not remember: are they a cause of anxiety? Why do you want to remember them? Is it because you feel guilty about not knowing them, or you think someone of your status should know about such things?

Getting interested in something becomes easier as one gets older. Why? Because:

- Unlike the novice or the young person, you have accumulated a bank of knowledge on which you can build; you are not starting from scratch with few landmarks to guide your new knowledge.

- You are clearer about what is important to you and what is not; choices and selectivity are easier.

- You are no longer on trial or have to pass exams; you can afford to say 'I do not know' about something.

SHORT-TERM MEMORY

Short-term memory is easily overloaded. For example, if you are listening to a speech or watching a movie and someone asked you to repeat word for word what you had heard in the last two minutes, you would probably find the task difficult: you were not paying attention to all the details. However, if the person were to ask you what the speech or movie was about, you would probably be able to reply quite easily. Paying attention to what you are doing is what short-term memory is about. As such, it has its limitations. George A.

Miller was the first psychologist to report that the mind can handle 'seven plus or minus two' concepts, letters, digits, as in telephone numbers, postal codes, anagrams, ideas central to a book, and so on without extra help like notes.

Short-term memory can be made more efficient if we reorganise or *chunk* the material. For example, if you are trying to memorise the contents of a manual, it will be easier and more productive if you memorise the titles or main ideas of chapters, say eight of them, rather than the first eight lines of important text in the manual.

Now fill each chunk with *meaning*. Meaning, as we discussed in Chapter 1, goes far beyond the visual recognition of words. Meaningful material relates to your past knowledge and experience, and expectations of what you want to extract. This is what experts call *encoding*. For example, can you name the Great Lakes of North America in 30 seconds? The answer (at the foot of page 56) shows how useful encoding is.

LONG-TERM MEMORY

Most people blame their long-term memory: recall is not as speedy as they would like, or as accurate, or it is simply not there. Long-term memory should be an organised, structured databank of knowledge, like the filing cabinet described earlier. It is organisation that makes retrieval and recall possible. There are many techniques available to help organise information, from using a diary to mastering mnemonics (an aid to memory).

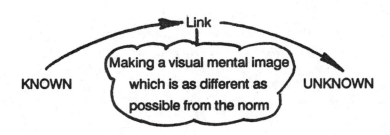

Figure 4.2 The Principle behind Mnemonics

Mnemonics

Mnemonics work on the principle shown in Figure 4.2. For example, take your house or flat (the Known). The purpose at the moment is to find ten different locations which are, to you, in a logical sequence. You may start with your front door. Mentally, re-acquaint yourself with it (take information in). Does it need repairing? Is the surface rough or smooth? Do you like it? Move to the second location, say the hall. Mentally re-acquaint yourself with it. If you switch the light on, is it bright or dull? Is the effect of the decoration pleasing? Warm? Is there an object there you particularly like? Now move to the third location, which to you is a logical sequence. Examine the room or place again, as before. Take your time.

Now, let's imagine that you need to memorise the contents of a report which has ten sections, say, Recession, Recovery, Interest rates, Unemployment, etc. Can you make a simple mental picture that represents each one? Recession could be an empty factory, while Recovery is a full order book. Now, all you need to do is to link the Unknown (the ten sections of the report) to the Known, your house. The first section is Recession, represented by an empty factory. Can you see your front door opening onto an empty factory? Now the second section, Recovery, represented by a full order book. Can you see in your hall, instead of a rug or a piece of furniture, a huge order book which people sign as they come in? And so on until you have linked the ten sections of the report to things you know well, in an order.

This memory aid technique has been in use since ancient Greek orators used it to memorise their speeches.

One Way to Describe Recall

Douglas Hofstadter, in his brilliant book Metamagical Themas: Questing for the Essence of Mind and Pattern (2), reminds us of the mathematician Stan Ulam's theory *about retrieval. When Ulam was searching for a piece of information that eluded him, he sent 'ten sniffing dogs' after it. The metaphor was to release the dogs in his brain and let them go sniffing in parallel. While some would go into the wrong alleyways, another would bring back the desired piece. Now have you not, on occasions, read something which you are trying to recall? And you say, hold on, it was last week, no, last month; that's right — I was on the train to Birmingham. Oh, I know, it was in that magazine about ... The dogs are searching and when they are on the wrong path you send them back. It is interesting that we need a small cue to retrieve the entire material. A whiff will do!*

Psychologists have long known that retention of knowledge decreases with time, particularly if the knowledge is not revised or used. The graph in Figure 4.3 illustrates how retention and recall ability decays. However, given the correct stimulus, we can remember everything. This shows that we retain perfectly what we do every day; the problem starts when we try to retrieve or recall this information.

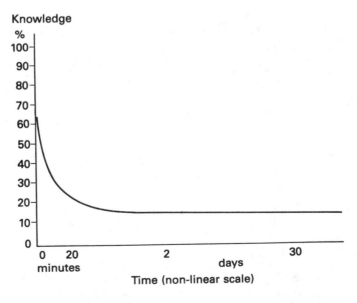

Figure 4.3 How retention and recall ability decays

Why do we forget? 'The easiest answer is, we don't,' writes Professor J. Z. Young (12). We have many subconscious memories. The problem lies in the fact that we have not yet mastered a system for retrieving them.

USE RECALL PATTERNS

To keep the information fresh in your mind, it helps if you use recall patterns. (Tony Buzan (13) calls them Mind Maps®.) The principles are simple:

* ★ Write the main idea or subject in the centre of the page.
* ★ Add associated ideas branching from the centre.
* ★ Use keywords which summarise a train of thought.
* ★ Write in capitals rather than in script to aid legibility.
* ★ Try to use a colour coding of related ideas, perhaps one colour per branch.

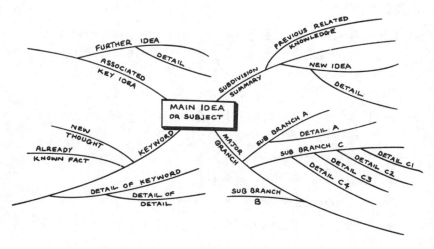

Figure 4.4 The Basic Mind Map®

The advantage of recall patterns over linear notes is that you organise the notes yourself and do not have to follow the author's plan. Thus it allows you to hook new pieces of information to old immediately, and enables you to tailor the information to the emphasis that you, rather than the author of the book, require.

HANDS-ON EXERCISES

PROCRASTINATION

☞ Reflect on the types of task you put off. Are they small tasks like filing? Or large like taking an important decision? What excuse do you use? How can you avoid the excuse?

INTERRUPTIONS

☞ Start a task: jot down how long it was before you were interrupted. Reflect how you could have avoided the interruption.

MEMORY

☞ Increase your interest by doing the following exercise. Look at a cup. Don't just say – 'Okay, it's just a cup – an ordinary cup.' Rediscover the cup for the next two minutes:

☞ If you hold it in your hand is it hot, cold, pleasing, rough, smooth?

☞ Is it greyish, yellowish ...?

☞ Does it have a rim at the bottom?

☞ Is it marked, chipped or crazed?

☞ Can you put one or two fingers through the handle?

☞ One hour later, without looking at the cup, recall all the features of the cup. Repeat the exercise the next day with a pen, a shoe and so on. Then a conversation you heard, a film you saw ...

Answer to question on page 52: using the mnemonic HOMES - Huron, Ontario, Michigan, Erie and Superior.

Part 2
Offence against Bumph

Chapter 5
Beat the Bumph

THE NATURE OF BUMPH PROBLEMS

WHAT TYPES OF INFORMATION SHOULD AN
ORGANISATION DISSEMINATE?

HANDS-ON EXERCISES

THE NATURE OF BUMPH PROBLEMS

The use of information technology – or the smart machine as some call it – is accelerating. But how instructive is the information or bumph you receive? Beware of dealing only with paper-driven information. Pay specific attention to computer technology-driven information.

Computerised information, computer-controlled production and computer-controlled stock-taking systems are here to stay. The emergence of information technology has reduced dramatically the cost of assembling, reproducing and disseminating information. Consequently, information has proliferated in many different formats such as magazines and periodicals, subscriber services, direct marketing, and cable and radio telecommunications facilities. You find you are on the mailing lists of organisations you never knew existed, bombarded with all sorts of offers, facts and data from all parts of the world. In your work you receive piles of information, much of which is of little or no use to you. Are you receiving information or bumph?

To take his first action against bumph, Ben uses the 'Bumph Log' shown in Table 5.1 to identify and eliminate unwanted material, and fills it in as illustrated.

To determine where your bumph problems lie, consider completing an analysis like Table 5.1. When you have given the Bumph Log some time and thought, you will be well on the way to analysing the problem and have some ideas on how and where it should be tackled.

First, from where do you receive information? Consider all types of paperwork, electronic and other information (and mis-information) that reaches your desk. We'll call all these information sources the **BUMPH.**

Second, with what **FREQUENCY** are you subjected to a particular type of bumph: several times per day or only once a year?

Third, what is your **NEED** for that bumph? How important is it to you? For example, you may be interested in only 10% of the contents of a particular computer database manual but that 10% is crucial for your job performance. So we have to weight the quantity estimate by describing the degree of

Table 5.1 Bumph Log Example

Here are some typical bumph items, frequencies, needs, quantities, purposes and times Ben has spent digging out required information. Add to or modify the list to maximise its usefulness to you.

BUMPH	FREQUENCY	NEED	QUANTITY	PURPOSE	TIME SPENT
Manuals	Annually	Crucial	10%	To operate PC	10 hours/year
Reports, internal/external	Quarterly	Very important	75%	Explore alternatives	6 hours/week
Memos	Weekly	Important	50%	Receive instructions	2 hours/week
Letters/post	6 per day	Sometimes	25%	Take action	10 hours/week
Meetings	Bi-weekly	Important	100%	Take action	6 hours/week
Minutes of meetings	Bi-weekly	Crucial	25%	Coordinate action	2 hours/week
Conference papers	Bi-annually	Sometimes	50%	Keep up-to-date	20 hours/year
E-mail	Daily	Crucial	75%	Keep up-to-date	5 hours/week
Books	6 per year	Sometimes	50%	Learn	20 hours/year
Professional magazines	Monthly	Sometimes	40%	Keep up-to-date	2 hours/week
Journals	Bi-monthly	Sometimes	10%	Keep up-to-date	2 hours/week
Newspapers	Daily	Low	25%	Keep up-to-date	2 hours/week
Computer printout	Daily	Important	1%	Disseminate info	1 hour/week

Table 5.2   *Bumph Log*

Make your own list. Review this list in, say, six months' time, to check how much you have improved your ability to deal with bumph.

BUMPH	FREQUENCY	NEED	QUANTITY	PURPOSE	TIME SPENT

importance of the information contained in the bumph source. So next to 'Need' we have **QUANTITY**, which denotes what proportion of a particular document is of use to you.

Next, we have to consider the **PURPOSE** for which you require the information. What arguments, ideas or actions will this reading prompt? Once absorbed, what will you do with this information? Will you mull it around in your head, prepare a presentation, incorporate it in a report, or give instructions?

And last, what **TIME** was **SPENT** working on each information source? How long did it take to dig out what you wanted from all the other irrelevant information?

Now complete your particular requirements on Table 5.2.

From your consideration of various types of bumph and their relative importance for you on the Bumph Log (Table 5.2), you should now have a good idea of which documents you should read carefully, look through quickly, or which you can ignore. Be assertive and bin (throw in the waste paper basket) unimportant documents or delete irrelevant computer monitor screen displays.

Do you see a bumph pattern emerging from Table 5.2, your own Bumph Log? If so, consult the list of bumph problems contained in the Introduction to this book. There you will find references to the answers.

WHAT TYPES OF INFORMATION SHOULD AN ORGANISATION DISSEMINATE?

As an information giver, how often do we think about what the reader will do with the information or data we are disseminating?

 Technical Bumph Case Study

In the 1970s computer manuals were written by boffins for boffins. They were so user-unfriendly (xenophobic) that they strengthened many people's fears about technology. Manuals are very different today. Their writers have learned the hard way that readers need to find information easily and that it

must be meaningful. This means that they help readers to bridge the gap between new data and previous knowledge, to feel encouraged and not overwhelmed, to find what they need quickly and not feel guilty about what they leave out. Here is an example of an improved manual:

'You should begin by reading Chapter 1 and trying some small exercises of your own. Go through Chapter 2 quickly, concentrating on the summaries and tables; don't get bogged down in details. Then read as far into each chapter as your interest takes you. The chapters are nearly independent of each other, so the order doesn't matter much.' (15).

Similarly with meetings: do you complain that you are wasting time because meetings are proliferating, the topics overlap, the chairperson or participants digress too frequently or the meeting goes on for too long?

What has happened with meetings and paper may happen on-line, with electronically controlled information. More businesses are using computers and related work-stations. As data collection, retrieval and dissemination are made easier through information technology, managers must restrain their appetite for more information, or work will soon drown in an excess of information.

But when you receive the 'correct' type of information your work performance can be revolutionised. Professor Zuboff, writing in *The Age of the Smart Machine* (5), argues that some organisations may use information technology not only to 'automate' but also to 'informate' workers. She means empower workers with knowledge. As one worker she interviewed put it: *'If I can control my own access to data, I can control my own learning'* (p 237). This means improved performance for the benefit of the organisation. Viewed this way, information becomes accessible to all and enables all personnel to learn and gain insight.

Some organisations are transforming organisational life through initiatives like empowerment. They are pushing responsibility and information down to all levels in the organisation and making people responsible for their own work performance, career, and personal growth. When people accept responsibility for their own access to and control of information, and share information wisely, they cut out the bumph.

A manager within an organisation must review the frequency, necessity and quantity of information that his team receives:

- Simplify and limit the information you generate and disseminate.
- Avoid any information that does not show a clear purpose.
- Scrutinise the need for formal meetings.
- Train people to run meetings efficiently.
- And remember, when was the last time you solved a problem by throwing data and statistics at it?

But it is a fine line between transmitting too much information and too little, as the following story illustrates.

> *J. Edgar Hoover, well known for the autocratic manner with which he ran the FBI in the 1930s and 1940s, was a master of handling information. He insisted that all memos for his attention should summarise the message on one (and only one) A4 size sheet, with wide borders left around the edges of the paper for his comments and instructions. He received one such memo, concerning spies, but the borders were a little narrow. Amongst his comments he included 'Watch the borders', meaning make sure the margins on the memo were kept wide. Immediately the telegraph wires were humming all over the United States. 'Watch the borders' went out the urgent instruction to all frontiers, ports and airports from his well-trained staff.*

 Retail Industry Case Study

Consider a large food retailer which sends daily, to each store manager, information covering about 100 A4 sheets. The information includes:

- *product lines discontinued and newly introduced*
- *errors on earlier information lists and on product labelling*
- *future special promotions and offers*
- *supply forecasts*
- *ordering advice*
- *health and safety notices and reminders*
- *limited availability of some products.*

Store managers have many responsibilities involved with the smooth running of the store, which they enjoy. This does not leave much time free for reading piles of bumph, which they do not enjoy.

If you were the director of information (information giver) what would you do to lighten the load on the store managers? To answer this question you need to put yourself into the position of a store manager (information receiver). You could:

★ colour code the information pages, so that pages concerning groceries may be handed directly to the groceries manager, health and safety to the H & S manager, and so on

★ prioritise information into immediate action items, and short- and long-term future action information

★ use a consistent set of icons on the information sheets to categorise items concerning, for instance, customers, errors, wrappings, internal communications, staff, reports, etc.

★ divide the A4 sheets into columns to ease reading, as a newspaper is laid out

★ check who really needs the information (i.e. prune standard distribution lists whenever possible) and who is the real recipient of the information. For instance, if it is a notice for the customer, send a notice already made out. Don't tell the store manager so that he has to have the notice made up.

HANDS-ON EXERCISES

☛ Keep a record of the nature of information sent to you. Develop a sense of criticism, and assess within the first three minutes of handling the document whether it will be of use to you, or whether some or all of it should be passed on to your team.

☛ Before you send information to colleagues, ask yourself: Why? How much will they need?

☛ Discuss with colleagues or subordinates the value of some meetings.

☛ As a manager, ask colleagues if or how information received has prompted some to make better or faster decisions. If not, why not?

☛ As a receiver of information, discuss with the sender how bumph (irrelevant information) could be stripped away from the information you really need to receive.

Chapter 6
Improve Your Reading

GET RID OF MYTHS ABOUT READING

ESTIMATE YOUR READING SPEED

CHECK YOUR COMPREHENSION AND READING HABITS

REDUCE THE EFFECTS OF DYSLEXIA

HANDS-ON EXERCISES

This chapter is concerned with anything that stops Ben getting to the information that he really needs. From his work in Chapters 1 and 5, Ben has gained an idea of the nature of the problems to be faced when dealing with bumph and reading effectively. In this chapter we consider how to overcome most of those problems.

GET RID OF MYTHS ABOUT READING

There are many myths surrounding the reading process.

READING FOR PLEASURE AND WORK HAS TO BE SLOW

There is no evidence to support this view at all. Slow readers, in fact, find pleasure reading too time consuming to be enjoyable. This, of course, makes such readers reluctant even to start. Slow reading discourages the reader because there are so few early rewards. Slow readers get a fragmented comprehension. They miss the overall driving idea and meaning of the material, in the same way as a copy-typist who necessarily reads every word may not take in what she types. Her mind wanders off because reading is at the pace of typing – slow and dull.

WHEN YOU FAIL TO COMPREHEND OR LOSE CONCENTRATION, IMMEDIATELY RE-READ

This is one of the most common faults of poor readers – going back to check what you have just read, to try to gain understanding. It is very inefficient. It slows you down. It allows your mind to wander off. It sidetracks you from anticipating what is coming. It distracts you from thinking actively.

A simple technique for increasing comprehension and concentration is to maintain a dialogue with the author. Ask questions: why did he say that? Is it different from what he said before? Anticipate what the author will say in the next section of the document.

READING IS BORING

This myth is popular with those who believe in myths 1 and 2. Reading is fun and rewarding if you are motivated, follow a rhythm and actively seek information. Reading fast, understanding it and retaining what is read are even more exciting.

SCANNING CAN'T BE READING

Scanning *is* reading. It is *the* technique to apply when you are looking for something specific and you want to gain an overview of a whole document. Scanning is taking mental note of the presentation of material, picking up what stands out and reading headings and keywords. It is a vital part of efficient reading, sometimes used by itself, but more often in conjunction with other steps (see Chapters 6 and 7).

YOU NEED LONG PERIODS OF TIME

You don't. If you know how to skim you can pick up ideas from any document, effectively, in five minutes. But efficient and rapid reading requires concentration. You need to concentrate as soon as you decide to read. When you know what your objectives are, reading can be done in five or fifteen minute slots. Long periods spent reading do not necessarily mean efficient reading.

TECHNICAL DOCUMENTS CAN'T BE READ RAPIDLY

Such documents lend themselves very well to rapid reading. In most cases they give background information which the reader may not need, at least to begin with. Efficient reading is a series of steps. The key step, in the case of technical reports, is to decide beforehand what you are seeking. Then scan the material, slowing down when you locate important passages. Of course, there will be more solid material in such documents than in a novel. To master the skill of efficient reading is to master flexibility — that is, use different speeds for different materials.

WHEN YOU READ, YOU NEED TO REMEMBER EVERYTHING

Put your efforts into making sense of the material. Over-anxiety about trying to remember it may damage your comprehension. Comprehension will take care of the need to memorise it.

This myth is a symptom of insecurity. You know it is an impossible task so you hide behind it. It allows you to say 'I told you it was impossible. I can't do it.' You need to set achievable targets. Assess your familiarity with the subject and define your goals for this reading.

YOU NEED TO BE AN EXPERT AT EVERYTHING

In a society that promotes education and bombards us with knowledge — be it legal, medical, political, or technical — we are afraid of appearing stupid. We pretend we know things we know little about and feel guilty if an area of ignorance is uncovered. Why? Resolve today to be selective. Remove the guilt. Remember that it is more important to know *where* to find information than to know everything.

ESTIMATE YOUR READING SPEED

How do you read? Let's find out. The passage which follows will assess the speed at which you read, the extent of your comprehension, and the habits that you have. For this exercise to be of full value, please follow the instructions:

- Have ready a stopwatch or a watch with a second hand.
- Choose a comfortable place to read where you will not be interrupted.
- Try to read as you would normally: don't speed up or slow down because it is an exercise.
- Have a notebook by your side.
- Note the time when you start and when you finish reading the passage.
- Read the passage once only, from 'Quote' to 'Unquote'.

Quote.

As brisk as bees, if not altogether as light as fairies, did the four Pickwickians assemble on the morning of the twenty-second day of December, in the year of grace in which these, their faithfully-recorded adventures, were undertaken and accomplished. Christmas was close at hand, in all his bluff and hearty honesty; it was the season of hospitality, merriment and open-heartedness; the old year was preparing, like an ancient philosopher, to call his friends around him, and amidst the sound of feasting and revelry to pass gently and calmly away. Gay and merry was the time, and gay and merry were at least four of the numerous hearts that were gladdened by its coming.

And numerous indeed are the hearts to which Christmas brings a brief season of happiness and enjoyment. How many families, whose members have been dispersed and scattered far and wide, in the restless struggles of life, are then reunited, and meet once again in the happy state of companionship and mutual good-will, which is a source of such pure and unalloyed delight, and one so incompatible with the cares and sorrows of the world, that the religious belief of the most civilised nations, and the rude traditions of the roughest savages, alike number it among the first joys of a future condition of existence provided for the blest and happy! How many old recollections, and how many dormant sympathies, does Christmas time awaken!

We write these words now, many miles distant from the spot at which, year after year, we met on that day, a merry and joyous circle. Many of the hearts that throbbed so gaily then, have ceased to beat; many of the looks that shone so brightly then, have ceased to glow; the hands we grasped, have grown cold; the eyes we sought, have hid their lustre in the grave; and yet the old house, the room, the merry voices and smiling faces, the jest, the laugh, the most minute and trivial circumstances connected with those happy meetings, crowd upon our mind at each recurrence of the season, as if the last assemblage had been but yesterday! Happy, happy Christmas, that can win us back to the delusions of our childish days; that can recall to the old man the pleasures of his youth; that can transport the sailor and the traveller, thousands of miles away, back to his own fire-side and his quiet home!

But we are so taken up and occupied with the good qualities of

*this saint Christmas, that we are keeping Mr. Pickwick and his
friends waiting in the cold on the outside of the Muggleton coach,
which they have just attained, well wrapped up in great-coats,
shawls and comforters. The portmanteaus and carpet-bags have been
stowed away, and Mr. Weller and the guard are endeavouring to
insinuate into the fore-boot a huge cod-fish several sizes too large for it
— which is snugly packed up, in a long brown basket, with a layer of
straw over the top, and which has been left to the last, in order that
he may repose in safety on the half-dozen barrels of real native
oysters, all the property of Mr. Pickwick, which have been arranged
in regular order at the bottom of the receptacle. The interest
displayed in Mr. Pickwick's countenance is most intense, as Mr.
Weller and the guard try to squeeze the cod-fish into the boot, first
head first, and then tail first, and then top upward, and then sideways, and then long-ways, all of which artifices the implacable cod-
fish sturdily resists, until the guard accidently hits him in the very
middle of the basket, whereupon he suddenly disappears into the
boot, and with him, the head and shoulders of the guard himself,
who, not calculating upon so sudden a cessation of the passive
resistance of the cod-fish, experiences a very unexpected shock, to the
unsmotherable delight of all the porters and bystanders. Upon this,
Mr. Pickwick smiles with great good-humour, and drawing a
shilling from his waistcoat pocket, begs the guard, as he picks
himself out of the boot, to drink his health in a glass of hot brandy
and water; at which the guard smiles too, and Messrs. Snodgrass,
Winkle, and Tupman, all smile in company. The guard and Mr.
Weller disappear for five minutes: most probably to get the brandy
and hot water, for they smell very strongly of it when they return,
the coachman mounts the box, Mr. Weller jumps up behind. The
Pickwickians pull their coats round their legs and their shawls over
their noses, the helpers pull the horse-cloths off, the coachman shouts
out a cheery 'All right,' and away they go.*

*They have rumbled through the streets, and jolted over the stones,
and at length reach the wide and open country. The wheels skim
over the hard and frosty ground: and the horses, bursting into a
canter at a smart crack of the whip, step along the road as if the load
behind them: coach, passengers, cod-fish, oyster barrels, and all: were
but a feather at their heels. They have descended a gentle slope, and
enter upon a level, as compact and dry as a solid block of marble,*

two miles long. Another crack of the whip, and on they speed, at a smart gallop: the horses tossing their heads and rattling the harness, as if in exhilaration at the rapidity of the motion: while the coachman, holding the whip and reins in one hand, takes off his hat with the other, and resting it on his knees, pulls out his handkerchief, and wipes his forehead: partly because he has a habit of doing it, and partly because it's as well to show the passengers how cool he is, and what an easy thing it is to drive four-in-hand, when you have had as much practice as he has. Having done this very leisurely (otherwise the effect would be materially impaired), he replaces the handkerchief, pulls on his hat, adjusts his gloves, squares his elbows, cracks his whip again, and on they speed, more merrily than before. Unquote.

This extract is taken from *The Pickwick Papers* by Charles Dickens, Chapter XXVIII, A Good Humoured Christmas Chapter. There are 1044 words in the passage.

Now let us consider how to calculate your reading speed. This is the formula to apply for this quotation passage:

Speed = (Number of words in passage)/(minutes)

Say you took 4 minutes and 5 seconds to read this passage:

4 min 5 sec = (4 + 5/60) = 4.083 minutes

Your reading speed = 1044/4.083 = 256 words per minute.

Or we can apply a general formula as another way to assess your reading speed. This approach is used when you read material that you have chosen, and you control the test reading time you wish to devote to it. You work out the average number of words per page from some sample pages where you have checked the typical number of lines per page and number of words per line.

Speed or words per minute = (words per line) × (lines per page) × (pages read)/(time)

or

Speed or words per minute = (words per page) × (pages read)/(time)

If you use this formula, you should select a reading time in advance and stop when it has elapsed. Choose 1, 2, 5 or 10 minutes for your test read. Use an alarm clock to tell you when the set number of minutes has elapsed. If you stop reading three-quarters of the way down the page credit yourself with three-quarters of a page read. If your passage has a lot of short lines, use your judgement to make up full lines, and estimate the fraction of a page that it fills.

CHECK YOUR COMPREHENSION AND READING HABITS

You are the best person to assess your reading comprehension. The questions to ask yourself about the passage you have just read (Dickens, *The Pickwick Papers*) to check your comprehension are:

- Have I got the general idea of what this passage was about?
- Is it sufficient for my present purpose?
- Am I missing some of the details? If so, does it matter?
- Do I understand enough of what I have read, so far, to continue?

For more mentally demanding 'reads' you may want to check some of the factors and techniques involved in improving comprehension by referring to the section on Reading and Understanding in Chapter 1.

In the passage from *The Pickwick Papers* that you read, did you notice any of the following habits:

- Hear the words in your head as you read (subvocalised)?   yes   no
- Read one word at a time?   yes   no
- Go back and re-read because you lost the meaning?   yes   no
- Have problems remembering what it was about?   yes   no
- Experience difficulty in maintaining your focus on the page?   yes   no
- Find that your concentration wandered off?   yes   no

If you have more than one bad habit — the number of 'yeses' in the list above — list them in order of their severity for you and go to the chapters in this book that deal specifically with them. Read only those sections that you do need to make you a rapid reader. Practice skimming now.

DO YOU HEAR THE WORDS IN YOUR HEAD?

Subvocalisation is hearing the words in your head, or saying the words to yourself as you read them. All readers do this to some degree. For example, if you are not a trained lawyer and need to read a contract, you will probably read it slowly, word for word. You are unfamiliar with the terminology and your eyes will take longer to recognise the words while your brain will be slower at decoding their meaning. *You may even read some words or groups of words aloud.* This is the extreme case of subvocalisation. If it is occasional and necessary for your understanding, do not worry about it. If, however, you subvocalise frequently, with familiar material, you have developed a bad habit and need to understand why.

When you learned to read, you said each word aloud to reinforce the relationship this particular order of letters conveyed as that particular word. Later, as you gained speed, reading aloud was discouraged. But some readers never lose this checking mechanism. They were not taught to modify their reading habits. They, particularly, were not taught to *read words in a group*, rather than singly. A fluent reader does not need to 'hear' the words to understand the meaning of what he or she reads.

Reducing subvocalisation is easy. If, for example, in the speed exercise you achieved a speed of 200 words per minute and you want to double it, you have to drop some subvocalisation. You simply must force yourself to read faster. Then you won't have time to 'hear' the words. At first you may feel a little disorientated. You will feel that you do not understand what you are reading. But persevere and trust yourself!

As you gain speed, you will find that you are converting the sounds into pictures — as images. We have the ability to visualise. When reading and visualisation are combined, your speed and your comprehension are high.

Examples of Subvocalisation

If you read in a foreign language, subvocalisation tends to occur more frequently than in your mother tongue. This is because at a young age you did not learn to read these sets of letters side by side. Consequently it takes longer for the brain to decode such letters and the words. For example, in 'les cheveux de cet enfant', 'les liens de parenté', 'votre lieu d'habitation', the letters 'eux', 'ien' and 'ieu', frequent in French, are rarely positioned side by side in English.

Similarly, if you embark on new studies or radically change jobs, you may be unsettled by new phraseology and terms. Subvocalisation may momentarily help you understand what you read.

In both cases — foreign language and a new vocabulary for you — decide first to familiarise yourself with as many new words as you can so as to lose their 'surprising' effect. When you think you have done so, force yourself to read faster and transform the words into images.

To practise visualisation, start with simple words. When you see the word 'house', picture in your mind a house. As you get better at visualisation, words describing abstracts will literally become shapes, colours or pictures in the same way as concrete words. For example, can you form a simple picture for partnership? How about two rings interlocked, or an elderly married couple? What about socialism? Perhaps a tall figure handing something to a smaller figure. Capitalism? Uncle Sam with bulging pockets! Visualisation is strongly linked to memory, see Chapter 4.

IMPROVE YOUR CONCENTRATION

 Case Study

Ben picks up the report he intends to read now. After a casual glance through it, he searches in his file for some background information which he reads. He gets up, goes to the window and comes back to his desk to make a phone call.

He now starts on the report, but it is heavy going. He thinks how dull and poorly presented this information is and misses important points. Ben looks at his watch and gets flustered because time is passing. He re-reads the last page he read and continues.

After twenty minutes or so, Ben stops reading because he has reached a particularly boring passage. He looks in his in-tray and quickly dictates two letters on his dictaphone. Ben closes the report and decides to go back to it after lunch.

After lunch, Ben flicks through the report again and thinks: pity that it has not changed in the meantime! How could Ben break this self-defeating cycle?

If you reach the bottom of a page and do not remember what you have read, your concentration is poor. You have allowed your mind to wander off; you have given in to distractions. External distractions can be greatly reduced if you minimise disruptions as suggested earlier. *Internal distractions* depend largely on your previous experience of reading similar documents, your general level of knowledge about the subject you are tackling and the nature of the material. People who tend to re-read paragraphs or pages because of poor concentration take the lazy way out. They are not consciously thinking about reading the first time round. To break this cycle you can:

★ refuse to re-read or regress as it is properly called.

★ read critically, with a purpose in mind. This is developed in Chapter 8, under Set Objectives.

★ use your power of anticipation. Try to anticipate the material you have yet to read. Try to foresee where the writer is taking you, how the report is progressing.

★ get involved. Don't read passively; have a dialogue with the writer, agree or disagree openly as you read.

★ don't fight your short concentration span: work with it. Every fifteen minutes, take small breaks. As you come back to the material, recall what you have read so far. Make some notes from memory.

Physical factors like the environment also affect concentration. Make sure that:

★ you read using daylight, whenever possible.

★ if you use electric lighting, it is neither too bright nor dull.

★ the ambient temperature is about 20 degrees Celsius.

★ you adopt a posture that puts minimum strain on muscles.

★ the chair supports your legs.

Finally, if you wish to improve your concentration in general, here are two exercises that you can practise at any time during the day.

☞ Look outside your window and focus on what is there. If you can, say aloud what you see. Give a judgement about the shapes or the colours; be precise and use adjectives to qualify the images. For example 'the greyish clouds seem to be in a hurry; the red car parked at the kerb could do with a wash; the grass looks freshly cut.' Make it last two minutes. Go back to your desk and try to recall what you saw.

☞ Take a watch with a second hand. It completes its cycle in sixty seconds. This exercise has three degrees of difficulty. First, watch the hand as it begins a new cycle and don't let your eyes wander from the moving hand. When you can watch one whole revolution without distraction you have overcome the first difficulty. Now, keep the focus as before, and at the same time count in your mind backwards from ten to one slowly so that you finish with one when the second hand completes its cycle. Do this several times, until it becomes less difficult. Finally, continue to watch the second hand while counting in your mind and repeat a nursery rhyme, or a piece of verse. How are you getting on? You may have to persevere...

REDUCE THE EFFECTS OF DYSLEXIA

Most poor readers have nothing intrinsically wrong. They simply find acquiring reading skills more difficult than learning, say, arithmetic or computer languages or music. However, some poor readers have an emotional or medical reason for their learning difficulty with reading. Dyslexia simply means the learning difficulty caused by a medical problem. The term 'learning difficulties' covers symptoms caused by emotional or linguistic problems and a variety of medical causes. 'Specific developmental dyslexia' is used when the problem can be medically categorised, and it is usually diagnosed in childhood due to the obvious symptoms (see McAuslan (6)).

Much progress has been made in the past few years towards an understanding of what dyslexia, is but there is an enormous amount still to be learned and understood. Dyslexia can vary from a very mild childhood form to one which continues to cause substantial difficulties throughout life. Dyslexia may be a consequence of partial deafness when young, or be induced by emotional tension or some brain malfunction. It is unlikely that anyone with a substantial degree of dyslexia would be reading this book.

But what of the person who has not been diagnosed as having a learning difficulty or dyslexia, but who privately has to struggle hard to keep up with their contemporaries?

First there is the obvious evidence of difficulty in learning reading skills. Then there might be more specific symptoms of dyslexia including an inability to distinguish left from right, or confusing objects with their mirror images. This is called 'crossed laterality'. It is manifest, for example, in confusing 'b' with 'd', or confusing the spelling of 'from' and 'form'. People with severe dyslexia may read 'puppy' as 'small dog', or 'Belgium' as 'Holland' (see Anthony Smith (7)). The characteristics common to these pairs of words indicate that the brain makes many correct associations, but fails to select the single correct word at the end of the reading/visualising/ recall process.

It is best for someone with a significant learning difficulty to seek professional help. But if you suspect you may have a mild form, you can help yourself to read faster by using a multi-sensory approach. You need to learn to read using, simultaneously, as many of your senses as possible. You acquire such a capability by drill. For example, here are a couple of very simple practices:

☛ The use of a guide – the finger as a pointer run vertically down the centre of the page at a reasonably fast speed – is one. The eyes are forced to follow the guide. This improves reading discipline and speed. (See Chapter 7 for details of 'pacers' to gain reading speed.)

☛ Moderately dyslexic people sometimes have erratic eye movements. A very simple visual aid, to train the eye to move horizontally, may correct this problem. The aid is a window or slot cut in the centre of a large postcard. The window is in the shape and size of one line of print. As the window is run down the page, the eye is limited to horizontal movements since the window shows only one line at a time.

Sensory assistance can help your reading in other ways. Link the words read (or groups of words) to as many sensory impressions as possible. Groups of words can be hooked on to images (little scenes described by the text) or your knowledge of the light, the sounds, the smell or touch of objects associated with the text you are reading. A young person may be helped if the observed scene is linked to reading. In the extreme, if a brown furry cat in the garden is crouching to catch a bird, the key words of the scene may be written down (possibly in brown ink), and by touching the cat (probably later) and smelling the garden (maybe the grass has been cut recently). In this way connections may be established between the words and other senses.

HANDS-ON EXERCISES

In this chapter there are exercises in the text. To be of long-term value these exercises should be repeated regularly, once a day or once a week.

Chapter 7
Improve Your Visual Skills

PREPARE FOR READING

YOUR INITIAL READING SPEED

MOTIVATION

EYE MOVEMENTS AND REGRESSION

PERIPHERAL VISION

USE A GUIDE

CONDITIONING: INTRODUCING RHYTHM

CONSOLIDATION

REST YOUR EYES

MAINTAIN YOUR SPEED

HANDS-ON EXERCISES

PREPARE FOR READING

Ben has admitted that he must change his reading habits if he wants to get through the bumph faster. He does not yet know how: that's what this chapter will tell him. And he will suspend his judgement until he has given the technique a fair trial.

This chapter gives you the techniques to increase your visual skills, to improve the dynamics of your reading. To familiarise yourself with the material and to learn to anticipate, browse through this chapter looking at the sub-headings, the diagrams, the summary at the beginning and the recommended exercises at the end. To work through the chapter, doing the exercises with a cooperative friend, should take about one hour.

This skill makes the same demands upon the learner as acquiring any other new skill, say skiing. Be child-like in your attitude. Children quickly sense the exhilaration of other children who can already ski. Their sole objective is to be able to enjoy themselves in the same way. They learn quickly because that objective is always before them. They accept short-term setbacks, like falling over. Being child-like means being unafraid of making mistakes. That is learning: finding out what works and what does not work. Children do not question the instructions. Today you are on the nursery slopes, with a limited speed and limited bumph-beating capability. No one will know of your mistakes as you learn to read rapidly. Look to the top of the mountain and be determined that you, too, will enjoy the thrill of speed.

Have a stopwatch or clock, a sheet of paper and a pencil by you. Use Table 7.1 or copy it on to the paper to record your progress. Ensure that your lighting is comfortable. Minimise the possible interruptions. Choose a comfortable chair and place it by a table. In some exercises below it is best if you have the help of a friend.

Now, select a book. As we are going to learn a skill together, it is important that we choose a book that is interesting and light. Go for a novel, avoiding 'classics' or humorous books. You are going in the shallow end of the pool for a few exercises, before you plunge in the deep end. It is better to tackle the technique with something that is easy to

Table 7.1   Results of reading exercises

Exercise	Speed	Comprehension
1 Initial reading		
2 Motivation		
3 Overcoming regression		
4 Peripheral vision		
5 Using a guide		
6 Conditioning		
7 Consolidation		

understand rather than multiplying the difficulties by adding deep philosophy (for which you may wish to stop and think) or strong humour (which needs laughter time).

New books, particularly paperbacks, should be 'broken in'. A book that wants to shut all the time is not helping you to read it. Place the book with its spine on the table. Open it at page 30. With the palm of your hand, press it hard open. Move your palm up and down the pages, against the spine so that the book stays open at that page. Repeat this process every 30 pages or so to the end of the book. Do not open the book in the middle, bending the covers backwards to meet: it breaks the spine of the book and the pages will fall out soon.

We will now proceed step-by-step, with a series of exercises to illustrate and practise each step. The overall objective is to make you a faster reader by improving your existing visual skills. That will mean building on what you already know, and perhaps changing one or two of your past habits. Now, think positively: you *can* read faster.

YOUR INITIAL READING SPEED

READING INSTRUCTIONS

Set yourself a reading time: two, three or five minutes and set your watch. Start reading the book, as you do normally. When the time is up, make a mark with your pencil where you stopped and calculate your speed, using the formula given in Chapter 6. Record your speed on Table 7.1. Also give yourself a mark between 0 and 10 to express your comprehension. This mark must reflect what you think you got from the reading. Do you have a good, general idea of what you read? Did you miss some bits or have you forgotten them already? Is it important? Can you go on? Evaluating comprehension each time you do a reading exercise will give you a rough idea of your reading progress. We will work on comprehension in more detail later.

The reading speed for the average English-speaking person is between 200 and 300 words per minute. If you are slightly below, let's say you are within the range. If you are above, you have a head-start. If you are very much below, you will have to pay attention to your faults and practise to correct them.

So, we are equipped with an initial or reference speed which we are going to improve.

MOTIVATION

READING INSTRUCTIONS

Your objective now is to *double* your reading speed. Whatever you achieved in the first exercise, aim to double it. To encourage you to do this, let's play a game. Suppose that if you double your speed you will win a superb prize.

Now, take the book again, and start reading from the last pencil mark. Read for the same amount of time as you did for Exercise 1. Mark the book with the pencil where you stopped. Note your speed and comprehension at Exercise 2.

You have achieved a higher speed than before or, indeed, you have doubled your speed. You have experienced motivation. Like Ben, you may be surprised that it was not very difficult. Motivation is the basic step that you have to apply every time you pick up something to read. But Ben feels rushed and fears he is missing something. To overcome this problem you, and Ben, need to:

★ Establish objectives or clarify your reading objectives.
★ Read in *short* bursts.

Before you proceed with other exercises, it will help you if you set an objective *now*. In the novel that you have started, are you going to follow the plot or the main character? You may be uncertain which to choose. Here are a few guidelines to help you.

★ If you are reading an adventure book with much action but characters are described simply and they do not change psychologically during the book, choose the plot.

★ If you are reading a story that evolves around people who are described in depth, perhaps one person emerges as a key character, at least for the moment: if it is likely that this character will change behaviour as the story unfolds, choose this character (even if you have to change character as you get deeper into the novel).

★ Do not choose both a character and the plot.

★ You may think there is a lot more in this book, style, atmosphere — yes there may be, but right now, ignore it. We will talk about that later in this chapter.

Setting objectives is essential for comprehension, and will make working on your visual skills easier. So before you read further, say 'My objective is to follow the plot', or whatever you decide.

EYE MOVEMENTS AND REGRESSION

Ask a friend to sit opposite you about one metre away. Hold your book up, so that he or she can see your eye movements over the book, while you read two or three lines. Ask your friend to describe the eye movements that he or she saw. View similarly the eye movements of your friend when she or he reads. Your descriptions will probably follow Figure 7.1.

The aim of this exercise is to observe the number of stops the eyeballs make per line. You need to be particularly observant here so that you can say to your friend 'Your eyes stopped four times, or six times per line.' It is not good enough to say 'Your eyes moved from left to right.'

In the figure, each balloon represents the eye resting on a word or group of words. In Figure 7.1 the eye goes forward five times, skips backward three spaces, then goes forward four more times.

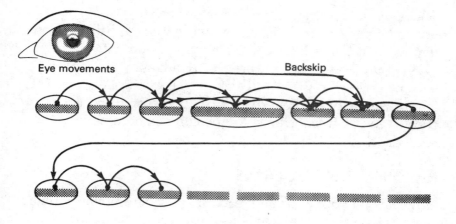

Figure 7.1 Untrained Eye Movements

That is, your eyes move with jerky movements or *saccades*, as these were first named. They take in a word or group of words and recognise the shape of the letters; the brain recalls the meaning of the word or words, then your eyes go on to the next word or group of words, and then to the next, and at each group the eye–brain process takes place. Now, the eyes may *go back* to check what was read before — perhaps because it is a foreign name or because the word is unfamiliar. Then the process starts again, until the eyes reach the end of the line and then ... zoom ... like an old-fashioned typewriter carriage, the eye starts again on the next line.

Every time the eyes stop on a word, it is called a *fixation*. Untrained eyes will fixate six to eight times per line. Every time the eyes go back to check on a word, it is called *regression* or *backskipping*.

A fixation can last from a split second to one second in very slow readers. One of the first things that you must try to do is to reduce the number of fixations to, say, three per line. And the first principle you are to put into practice is to eliminate regression. This will help you to read smoothly. The smoother your eye movements, the faster you read. Can you also be aware of a sense of rhythm?

Why do you regress? Because you are unsure of what you read and think that you have missed something important.

That may be true, but it is inefficient. There are two possibilities: either it is important and the author will mention that word again, or it is not, so why worry about it?

As you go on and pick up speed, avoiding regression will become easier: the speed will make you concentrate more. This in turn will heighten your overall comprehension and will encourage you to anticipate. Regression will become redundant.

READING INSTRUCTIONS

Now pick up your book and read for the same amount of time as you did before. Your aim is to go faster than last time. *You will achieve this by reducing the number of fixations per line and by avoiding regression.* Mark your book with a pencil where you have stopped. Calculate your speed, and record speed and comprehension against Exercise 3. Ben is pleased that this is not difficult to achieve and says that as he is becoming more familiar with the names, regression is unnecessary.

PERIPHERAL VISION

Sit opposite a friend, about a metre apart. Have your friend hold his or her index fingers, tip touching each other, between your faces, at the distance from you where you normally hold a book. Your friend will now move his or her fingers apart, horizontally, slowly. You must look at his or her eyes, not fingers. When one of the fingers goes out of your field of vision tell him or her to stop moving it. Do the same on the other side. Now look at the space between the two fingers. Repeat the exercise with the fingers moving vertically. See Figure 7.2.

You can determine your peripheral vision by yourself if you stare at one letter in a line of print. Place a finger on the letters each side of it. Then move the fingers apart until you can no longer recognise the recently uncovered letters. The distance between the fingers is probably wider than you expected. It represents your peripheral vision. You should be able to see and understand five average words in a group. You use peripheral vision every day; when you drive, for example.

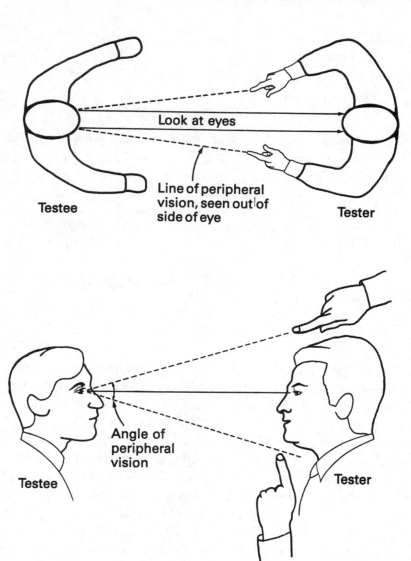

Figure 7.2 Peripheral Vision Assessment
by permission of Tony Buzan

Without moving your eyes, you notice that a light is changing colour, a child is about to run across the road, and so on. All the while you are concentrating and looking straight ahead.

When it comes to reading, however, you make little use of this peripheral vision if you look at only one word at a time. Focus your eyes on a particular word in a line of print, then try

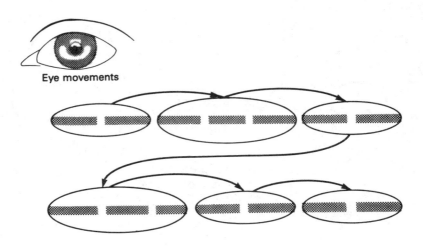

Eye movements

Figure 7.3 Eye Movements Using Peripheral Vision

to read the words on either side. With training you can 'take in' several words at a time (in one fixation) so that you now read as shown in Figure 7.3. Note that the eye focuses on larger groups of letters or words than before. The eye goes to the centre of each balloon and uses peripheral vision to see the characters which fill the distance between the centre and the edge of each balloon. Thus a few centimetres at each end of the line are read by using peripheral vision, and now the eye is moving a shorter distance from left to right than it was before.

As peripheral vision is so useful it is worth exercising to improve it. Draw a vertical line down the middle of a page of text. Then focusing only on the vertical line, at the first line of text see how many letters are seen to either side of the vertical line. Move down the vertical, and the number of letters seen by the peripheral vision will increase with practice.

a	c
wy	zo
nip	zag
acts	uvwy
and so	on and

If you don't make peripheral vision work for you, you waste a lot of effort and energy reading blank margins, at both ends of each line!

READING INSTRUCTIONS

Now take your book again, at the last pencil mark, and start reading. Remember to follow plot or character, to take in larger groups of words in one fixation, and to read faster than before. You will achieve this by starting to read two or three words into the line and stopping two or three words before the end of each line. Read for the same time as before.

When you have finished this reading exercise, mark the book with a pencil to note where you stopped, calculate and record your speed at Exercise 4. Your speed may have gone down. There is no cause for alarm. This is a learning process, and learning is made of highs and lows. Just remember the first time you climbed on to a bicycle: you probably concentrated on watching the front wheel and kept falling off until, as if by magic, it all came together – posture, movement, looking up straight, and you were speeding down the road, probably unable to stop and get off safely.

This exercise proved more difficult for Ben to sustain. He was tempted several times to return to the beginning of each line. As he caught himself, he lost the sense of what he had read which was frustrating. At the end of the exercise, though, a rhythm began to appear.

USE A GUIDE

Sit opposite your friend again, and ask him or her to draw a circle in the air or with his or her eyes, i.e. follow the circumference of an imaginary circle which may be around your head. Observe the eye movements and describe what you saw. Probably the eyes moved following a shape like that shown in Figure 7.4.

Now, guide your friend's eyes with your finger, by drawing an imaginary circle in the air. Your friend's eyes follow the finger. Observe your friend's eyes again. Their movement now is smoother, like that shown in Figure 7.5.

This suggests that, to help your eyes move smoothly on a page, and to avoid wandering off and regressing, you need to guide your eyes when you read. Initially, the guide will take your eyes along each line, and down the page, line by line. This is something that you already do. If you are suffering from toothache you take the telephone book to look for the telephone number of your dentist. You use your finger to search down the column for the correct name and number. Why? Because you are in pain and are trying to save time as well as not wishing to make an incorrect call. You are motivated.

So, from now on, use a finger or the tip of a pencil as a guide – whichever feels comfortable when you read. A finger is recommended because usually you have it with you and thus you have no excuse for not using it while reading!

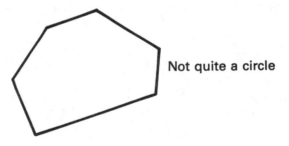

Figure 7.4 Unguided Eye Movements

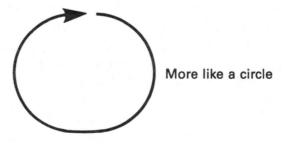

Figure 7.5 Guided Eye Movements

Figure 7.6 Using a finger as a reading guide or pacer

READING INSTRUCTIONS

Let us put this into practice. Take your book again and start reading, for the same amount of time as before, starting at your last pencil mark. Remember to apply *motivation*, that is to read faster than before, to follow your *objective*, to avoid *regression*, and to *group the words* — fixating, say, twice or less per line, to avoid reading from margin to margin. Use your finger while you read for this exercise (Figure 7.6).

Mark your book where you have stopped, calculate your speed and record both speed and comprehension at Exercise 5 — Using a guide.

Ben is amazed: his reading speed and comprehension went up. If you are like Ben, move on to the next exercise. If you think the finger or pencil slowed you down, then move it faster!

You may also have found the guide a distraction, or that using it felt strange. Don't give up: persevere. You are not used to using a guide systematically, as you have just done. With practice, the guide will help you to gather speed and will focus your concentration.

> ### Can you swim or do you run?
>
> *An analogy may persuade you. Imagine that you have joined a swimming or running club and that you practise once or twice a week with your fellow members. In swimming people practise in lanes, depending on their speed. Very quickly, you know which person you like to follow and which other person you do not like to follow. Those swimming too slowly are infuriating because you keep catching them up. It destroys your sense of rhythm. Those swimming too fast exhaust you. You need to put in too much effort to keep the same distance and your rhythm is also upset. Similarly runners have pacers to follow.*
>
> *In reading, the guide is the ideal person in front of you: it is slightly ahead of where you are reading; it prompts you to go faster, it allows you to maintain a comfortable rhythm.*

CONDITIONING: INTRODUCING RHYTHM

Some people have an innate sense of rhythm and find it easy to apply. One way to start is to move along the lines following your heartbeats, so that your finger (or pencil) traces one line per heartbeat. Do this for a page or two.

Now try to increase the pace either by saying 'line, line, line' to yourself, or by using a metronome set at a speed slightly faster than is comfortable. Do this for two pages, or until it feels natural.

We are now going to practise high-speed reading with rhythm. You are going to read from your last pencil mark, using a guide and rhythm. Start at a comfortable pace and then progressively speed up until you cannot move your guide fast enough to keep up with the rhythm. At this point you will have to zig-zag down the page tracing a maximum of three zig-zags per page (see Figure 7.7).

To practise conditioning correctly, you need to hold your book correctly, with your left hand at the top of the right-hand page to turn the pages, while your right hand does the zig-zag movements, if you are right handed. If you are left handed and

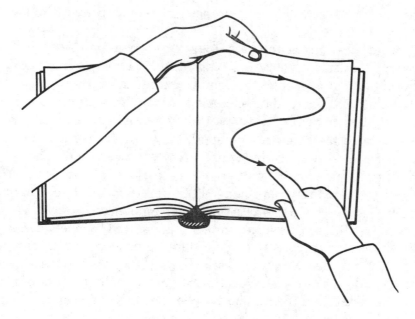

Figure 7.7 Fast Reading Conditioning with Rhythm

using your left hand as your reading guide, turn the pages with your right hand, so that the rhythm is maintained.

Set your watch for five minutes now and start from the last pencil mark. Remember that you are constantly speeding up, moving down the pages very fast to end up at the rate of about one page per second. You may experience a blur during the exercise. This is normal. Your eyes need to adjust to this new way of receiving and sending the information to the brain. To keep your motivation, start to look for keywords on each page. If you take in half a dozen words you are doing very well. Start now, and get hooked on speed!

READING INSTRUCTIONS

We are not going to record this speed — it was a practice exercise. Go back to your last pencil mark, the one you made at the end of Exercise 5. Set your watch for slightly longer than before and start reading, using all the techniques you have learned so far. Read, going as fast as you can with some comprehension.

When the time is up, mark your book where you have stopped, calculate your speed and record it under Exercise 6, Conditioning, on Table 7.1. Ben has exceeded his own expectations. His reading speed is a lot higher. Why? Because shortly before he read, he conditioned himself to read faster.

Like an athlete before a competition, you have warmed up your muscles to be ready for use when you need them. The rhythm became natural and your eyes got used to moving rapidly, following your guide. Although you read more slowly in this last recorded exercise, you were influenced by the high-speed conditioning. We are similarly influenced by speed when we drive on a motorway at a constant 70 miles per hour for a long time. When we want to take the sliproad marked clearly at 40 mph, we rarely slow to this: we brake a little, convinced that we are doing the required speed. The actual speed is probably more like 50 mph and that seems very slow!

Ben is worried about his comprehension, which is only sketchy, and wonders how it can be improved.

If your reading speed is considerably improved, well done! Now, let us look into comprehension more carefully: we must bring *speed* and *comprehension* into unison. If your comprehension is adequate, skip the next few lines and go on to the next exercise. If your comprehension is low, let us check a few things:

★ Are you clear about your objective, what are you following – plot or character?

★ Do you keep this in mind while you read?

★ Do you move your guide smoothly underneath the lines of your page?

★ Do you look for keywords along each line?

If you answer 'yes' to all these, then slow down. At this stage, there is no point in having speed for speed's sake.

If your answer is 'no', then pinpoint where you are going wrong and alter your habits. Then repeat the last exercise.

The speed used in the conditioning exercise is the speed you will apply when you overview a document quickly; this is described in Chapter 8. It is important that you understand the value of conditioning, practising zig-zagging to enhance your concentration and speed. Once you have experienced this several times, it becomes a habit and a necessary step to recognising quickly what you need in a document. It is only when you have mastered conditioning that you can claim to read faster and with flexibility: high speed to overview and a more leisurely speed – a cruising speed – to read what really interests you.

CONSOLIDATION

READING INSTRUCTIONS

Take your book and begin to read from the last pencil mark. Read to consolidate everything we have learned so far. We are now trying to bring speed and comprehension together. Relax. Do not worry about technique: you have mastered it. Enjoy your book. Probably you will need to slow down. Do so. Aim to double your initial speed, with a comprehension estimate of 7 or 8. To achieve this be flexible when you read: you now have a range of speeds to choose from. Use them. When the story interests you (it depends on your objective), slow down. When it does not, or it is repetitive, speed up. Do not skip – that is not reading – but get a general idea, perhaps using your highest speed.

How does Bel drive her car?

Bel wanted to drive to Scotland. Her aim was to get there quickly. The motorway was the obvious route. Almost always in top gear, she got there quickly.

Once arrived, one morning she wished to explore the area. She took the scenic route and found herself admiring the countryside, using the gear lever frequently around the bends, avoiding sheep, in second or third gear. She enjoyed the ride. Later that day she made her way back to the hotel and she took the straight rapid road.

Bel had used the gears and speeds of her car to fulfil her needs.

Like Bel driving her car, the speeds that you have mastered with your novel are now able to be used. Your final overall speed will be an average. Vary your speed according to what is in front of you. Do not become the prisoner of one speed.

Read for at least five minutes. When this time is up, mark your book where you have stopped, calculate your speed and record it under Exercise 7, Consolidation. Ben is pleased: he has doubled his reading speed. He think that with practice he could triple it. His comprehension is high, about 8 out of 10. A great feeling of achievement.

Your reading should be more stable now. You have *motivation*, you have an *objective*, you are eliminating *regression*, you are *grouping* the words, you are using a *guide* to help you focus and concentrate, you can *speed up*.

If you are still having difficulties, which is not uncommon at this stage, repeat exercises where you find difficulty. Learning a skill is unpredictable: some wonder why they did not take it up sooner, others stumble here or there and take a little longer. Remember you only started to read faster an hour or two ago. All this is new and you are changing some habits that have been with you for many years.

REST YOUR EYES

You may have found these exercises tiring for your eyes or you may experience tired eyes without trying to read faster. Here are two exercises to rest your eyes.

☛ Put your elbows on a table. Shape your hands into small cups in which you are going to rest your eyes. The word 'rest' is important. Do not apply pressure to the eyeballs as this would make the exercise useless. You should feel comfortable.

Close your eyes and create a picture. Imagine that you are standing in a large golden-yellow cornfield. It is a sunny summer day. Look all around you. Look to the left. There is a tall poplar rising to the sky. Look at it from the trunk up; look at the green leaves against the blue sky. In the sky, on the right, there is a plane cruising from the right to the left. Now look at your feet: there are poppies, bright red poppies and in the distance, far away, on the right there is a church spire that rises on the horizon. Look at the whole scene again: the golden-yellow corn, the tall green tree, the blue sky and the plane moving from right to left, the red poppies at your feet and the church spire in the distance. Remember that all this should be done without feeling any pressure on your eyes.

When you take your hands away and open your eyes, things around you are much brighter and your eyes feel refreshed.

☛ Another simple exercise is to focus on a far point – ideally out of a window. Hold the position for five seconds and then, without moving your head, focus on the nearest point in the room and maintain your focus for two or three seconds. Repeat the exercise five times.

Both these exercises require that you move the muscles that surround your eyes. You move them sideways and up and down. It helps to keep your eyes in good shape. Visualising colour in the dark also has a restful effect. These exercises do not take long and are particularly beneficial if you work in artificial light (see W. H. Bates (10)).

MAINTAIN YOUR SPEED

When you feel that you have mastered the technique of reading faster while maintaining comprehension (and it may take a little longer than doing the seven exercises), how do you keep your new skill?

You will need to practise about five minutes every day. One recalls here the words of a ballerina: 'If you do not practise one day you notice it. If you don't practise for two days, the public notices it!' The practice takes the form of high-speed conditioning. The best material to practise on is a newspaper, because it has narrower columns and therefore you need only one fixation per line. Also, as a rule, a newspaper article, such as a leader, summarises a situation with which you are already familiar. It is easy to read quickly, until you come to new information or opinion, at which point you will slow down, but still keep a fast rhythm.

You may be wondering how fast should I read? There is no limit. What you feel is comfortable becomes the norm. Remember that flexibility is synonymous with rapid reading, and that to get at what you want quickly is as important as reading and absorbing the information.

If you wish to go faster still, start the process again, in a step-by-step manner, as we have done through this chapter, focusing on speed first and comprehension later.

But, I hear you say, there *is* more to my book than the plot or character. In this case adopt the 'Book Reviewer Technique'. Many reviewers first read a book at a speed of 600 to 800 words per minute to see what the book is about. Once they know, they will read the book again, this time concentrating on, say, the credibility of characters, at the same speed. Now, if the book is well written, they will read the book again at that speed but looking at the English and enjoying it.

In other words, read the book with only *one* purpose in mind. If the book is worth it, it is better to read it two or three times at a good speed than once slowly, trying to follow everything at the same time.

HANDS-ON EXERCISES

To practise getting information fast, look at a poster or a notice on a notice board for only three seconds, then:

☛ Look away and ask yourself —
- was this pleasant to read or easy to grasp?
- what was the document colour and typeface?
- could I describe the picture (trees or three paragraphs)?
- could I give details about the picture (trees were tall and thin, the sky had clouds on the right, or the typeface was small and one heading had an exclamation mark)?

☛ Look back at the picture or notice to check what you had learned from your quick glance and what you had missed.

☛ With practice you will learn more and more from similar quick glances.

Practise conditioning reading a newspaper. The narrow columns make it easy for the eyes to speed down them. Give yourself a time limit. Check your speed.

Chapter 8
Six Steps to Systematic Reading

TREAT A BOOK AS A WHOLE

THE SIX STEPS TO SYSTEMATIC READING

WHY WAIT UNTIL THE END TO MAKE NOTES?

FLEXIBILITY IN READING

A TYPICAL DAY AND THE SIX STEP APPROACH

HANDS-ON EXERCISES

TREAT A BOOK AS A WHOLE

Take a look at Figure 8.1. The dots perhaps have no meaning for you. However, once you know that a Dalmatian dog is in the picture, you are able to find it since we all have a mental pattern of a Dalmatian dog.

Books have patterns too. The pattern is obvious in fiction, where a story-line is built around a hero and you follow him or her through various exploits and sub-plots. This concept of pattern is what is meant by 'wholeness'. The author had a plan and your first task for any reading material — a book, a report, an editorial or newspaper article — is to discover the author's plan. Rapid reading of a book requires you to refer to and consider the material as a whole, to consider that book's plan — and you must know that plan!

Figure 8.1 What Pattern Fits This Picture?

THE SIX STEPS TO SYSTEMATIC READING

You have a book to read. These six steps are the systematic approach to reading a book.

1. RECAP: BRUSHING UP YOUR MIND

Purpose

This is a warm-up exercise, similar to that carried out by an athlete before a competition. It also helps the reader start to identify gaps in his or her knowledge.

Method

Consider the title and jot down a few keywords describing what you know about the subject. This memory search puts you in a positive mode and prepares you to connect new information to the knowledge you already possess. People sometimes say that they know nothing about a subject. This is rarely true. Because of the quantity of information people are bombarded with through the media, through travel, through conversation, is there anything so utterly new that one's mind is an absolute blank? Remember what was said in Chapter 1: 'Reading faster is first an attitude'. This positive attitude starts here. We gain motivation.

Timing

This step should be done quickly, spending no more than two minutes.

2. SET OBJECTIVES

Purpose

An analysis of your objectives increases your concentration and helps you to achieve them. It also boosts your confidence and helps you to speed up.

Method

This *most important* step applies to all reading material. What are you reading it for? This seems obvious. Yet those who complain that they do not 'get on' with reading, or that they have to read every word, or that they get bored, do so because they did not spend a few minutes establishing their personal objectives. It is the corner-stone that makes your reading more efficient and memorable.

'A man without a goal is like shooting a gun without a target'
                                                        Benjamin Franklin.

If you don't know what you are looking for, how can you find it? A book, particularly a textbook, contains a lot of information. It caters for a variety of people and the author does not know who the reader may be. So the author develops some basic ideas, and links these to more sophisticated ones. It is the reader's job to choose what he or she needs and to concentrate on those parts, leaving the rest aside. When you establish your objectives, trust your own existing knowledge and feel confident.

How do you set objectives? By formulating one, two or three questions. Questions force you to look for answers and help you to keep focused. For example, when you began to read this book, the questions you asked yourself might have been:

★ Will this book help me to read long office reports rapidly? (See this chapter.)

★ Will I be able to read fiction twice as fast? (See Chapter 7.) or

★ Will I be able to stop moving my lips when reading? (See Chapter 6 on subvocalisation.)

Again, you must ask yourself what you want. Do you want to improve your reading or information absorption ability? Is it familiarisation with the subject, deep understanding of the ideas, or reinforcement of your knowledge that you seek?

Bad Objectives

'If you do not know what question to ask, you do not comprehend what you are doing' writes Frank Smith in his book *Reading* (3). Be specific when you set out your questions. Avoid all-embracing phrases such as 'get an awareness of' or 'acquire knowledge about', which is a common mistake among poorly motivated readers. Focus each question on a clear topic.

Sometimes people confuse Reading Objectives with Thinking Objectives. For example a reader may ask:

- 'Will this help my research?'
- 'Do the recommendations apply to us?'
- 'What do I need to do?'

These are *Thinking Objectives*. The reader can decide whether the material will help (or that it applies to them, or that they had to do this or that) only *after* they have absorbed what the document is about. The purpose of efficient reading is to get through documents faster so that you have more time to THINK about the information you have absorbed. It is not to read more.

Well-formulated objectives, combined with good visual skills, will give you more time for more important things than reading.

Making the Pips Squeak

Why not give yourself a time limit as well? For example:

- 'Can I, in 10 minutes, familiarise myself with x, y and z?'
- 'Can I, in 30 minutes, outline X's arguments on Y?'
- 'Can I, in 20 minutes, summarise the Board's recommendations about the new computer system?'

Giving yourself a time limit allows you to measure your progress, keep an awareness of time and a concentrated mind.

Timing

Don't set yourself unreasonable tasks. No more than five minutes.

3. OVERVIEW

Purpose

This gives you the feel of the book. You start to locate the information you seek and you decide whether the book is worth reading.

Method

Using the high-speed conditioning learned in Chapter 7, do an overview of the whole book. Pay attention to whatever stands out. This will include the cover, the table of contents, the index, the introduction, the summaries, the tables, diagrams, illustrations, chapter headings and bullets (●) it contains. Flick through it very rapidly. This is not reading in the ordinary sense but looking at the structure, presentation and contents of the book. This is scanning a document, literally looking at the whole. If you can, make a mental note of where what you want (your objectives) is located in the book.

Timing

Take five minutes for this exercise, literally flicking through the pages.

4. PREVIEW

Purpose

Preview keeps you focused. It is the art of rejection and keeps you from becoming sidetracked and distracted by irrelevant information (bumph).

Method

Strike out, using a pencil, those parts of the document that do not meet your objectives. This also means rejecting bumph: repetition, padding or information that is already familiar. A glance, looking roughly four lines at a time, tells you whether a paragraph, a page or even a whole section contains the information you are seeking. It is not easy to do, as we are reluctant actively to discard what someone has written. But it is essential if you are to keep to your objectives. When you hesitate, look again at the objectives. Be ruthless in eliminating whatever is not relevant. When your objectives are well defined, it is easy; with practice, it comes naturally. This is skimming – reading superficially.

Timing

Again, read as quickly as you can. The time will vary with the type of material, the way it is presented and according to how well you defined your objectives. A time for a typical book might be ten minutes.

5. INVIEW

Purpose

Inview provides you with detailed understanding.

Method

You have identified the points that interest you. You are focused and ready to read in depth. Read with comprehension in mind. Read line by line. If you have problems with comprehension, keep going: the answer may be on the next page. Continue to treat the material as a whole, building up knowledge as you read.

Your speed will depend on the nature of the book. It is important to keep a flexible approach. Use a pencil or highlighter to mark key ideas or key words. Now is the time to apply the rhythm and cruising speed we learned in Chapter 7. Try to keep a good speed, a 'tempo', where you are moving along comfortably, but under slight pressure.

If at the end of this in-depth reading you have gaps in your comprehension, read the book again. It is surprising how much better comprehension and retention are if you read, rapidly, the same material two or three times rather than slogging through once, stopping at every difficulty. So, when you have a problem, make a mental note or mark the page and continue. Return to the problem later, if necessary.

Timing

Set yourself a realistic time for this task and stick to it. In Steps 1 to 4 you cut out lots of unnecessary reading. Now you can be generous (20–30 minutes) to ensure you achieve your objectives.

6. REVIEW

Purpose

To check that all objectives are met and to reinforce retention.

Method

To consolidate what you have read, you must link it to your previous knowledge. Make a Mind Map®. This enhances long-term memory because you hook new information on to what you already know. It is also early use of this new material which means that it will become part of your knowledge. Review is also a way to check whether any fuzzy areas remain which you may need to go back to briefly later. The Mind Map® is the way to summarise and link ideas. Do it from memory. If you have information gaps, refer to your document and fill in these gaps with a different colour.

Timing

Depending on the amount of detail, a typical time for one book may be ten minutes, but you may need longer.

WHY WAIT UNTIL THE END TO MAKE NOTES?

Make notes at the end of all the reading steps. This makes you selective about the information you choose to keep.

Do not make notes from the text as you read. These notes will reflect the sequence of ideas as you read them. It is inefficient because:

- It is time consuming.
- The notes will be unnecessarily bulky.
- It encourages mental laziness.
- It does not indicate that you are absorbing what you read.
- The notes may not be necessary.

Notes made after all the different reading steps contain what the document means to you. It is now part of your mental property or knowledge. To ensure long-term retention of it you need to link it to what was already in your memory. In order to do this, you will probably use a different layout or sequence from that used in the book because the information is yours and fits into your experience.

Also writing and reading are two different activities, requiring different mental and physical actions. When they are mixed, each interrupts the other as you go back and forth between them and this disturbs your reading rhythm. When they are separated, they reinforce each other.

Now, if we apply this idea to the passage we read from *The Pickwick Papers*, we can summarise it as shown in Figure 8.2. The Mind Map® is made around the three main subjects. Unfortunately they do not evoke the atmosphere presented by Dickens' prose. Thus it is important to highlight and remember that Mind Maps® do not replace linear writing! However, from these notes you could easily tell a friend – or an audience – about the passage. The asterisks (*) show the links between subjects.

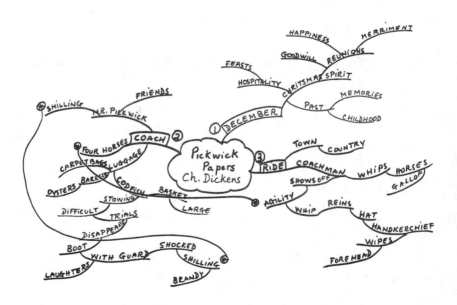

Figure 8.2 Mind Map®: *Pickwick Papers*

FLEXIBILITY IN READING

Although we have been through a systematic approach to the reading of books, there are differences between individuals and between the documents they handle. Some steps can be omitted. We are going to have a look at specialised reports and put this to the test in the next chapter.

Learning to read faster is like learning to cook. First you learn the rules. You must acquire some basic principles like how to cook green vegetables or red meats; then you refine this knowledge with the elements for simple sauces. Once you have *got the basics*, and *understand why* things are done this way, you can *adapt* any recipe to your own taste, what feels right for you. So you must follow the rules until they become second nature. When that stage is reached, you can skip a stage, or combine two, just as you would with your favourite dishes – add more salt or substitute for the cream to suit your needs and the ingredients that are available.

Above all, be flexible.

A TYPICAL DAY AND THE SIX-STEP APPROACH

At this stage we need to consider the style of Bel's office life before she adopts the techniques recommended in this book.

> ### Does Bel's Situation Sound Familiar?
>
> *When Bel gets to her office, usually by 8:30 each morning, she wonders whether she will achieve some of her personal objectives. Bel is at present the manager of a team of six, on a project which is to last 18 months. She has been asked recently to give a one-day workshop as part of an in-house training programme. Part of her job is to write company procedures and guidelines, which are to be incorporated into proposals. Each of these roles requires keeping up to date with what is going on in a particular field. In the last three months, Bel has found herself attending more meetings, receiving more reports, and generally having to cope with more information than ever before.*

Bel has tried dealing with each piece of paper as it arrives. But frequently this is not possible. The phone rings with an urgent query, the information required is not obtainable immediately or the sheer amount of paper is too much to handle in one go.

She has tried making piles. Unfortunately, the piles mount up rapidly and become an embarrassment, with colleagues asking for documents which need to be circulated.

In desperation, Bel has taken reading material home. She feels guilty that this is the wrong time to tackle paperwork, and more often than not, reports and journals are carried back and forth in her briefcase without as much as a glance!

How did Bel help herself?

THE TWICE-A-DAY, ONCE-A-WEEK AND TWICE-A-YEAR PRINCIPLE

First, as the post is distributed each morning and each afternoon, Bel sorts it into piles:

- *Pile 1* contains letters and memos which require immediate attention and action, or which can be answered – or delegated – right away, and *she does so at the time*. If there may be a delay and the incoming document may float around her desk for more than a day, then she puts it, together with any related notes or letters, in a transparent plastic folder. The folder acts as a reminder that it must be dealt with very soon.

- *Pile 2* contains documents which require some time to be read, or documents which can only be dealt with after more information is assembled.

Second, Bel sets a day in the week in which she will do her serious reading (Pile 2), and makes this a routine. Ideally this is first thing in the morning, so that she benefits from natural lighting and a refreshed mind. A rule of thumb is to devote two hours per week. If possible, Bel closes the door, redirects the telephone, eliminates distractions and does her reading *uninterrupted*, using the six-step approach.

Third, twice a year, Bel goes through her long-term filing system. She has clipped articles, kept reports or booklets which are no longer accurate, nor relevant to her job. She gets rid of 70% of this material by throwing it away, passing it to colleagues to whom it may be useful, or sends it back to the Central Filing system.

There may be a document that has to be read that day and between other tasks. So how does Bel proceed?

Say it is 9 o'clock and someone hands a report to Bel saying that he would value her opinion on it. Bel has a meeting at 9:15 and thus cannot devote much time to it. If the topic is unfamiliar, or Bel finds it hard to motivate herself to read it, she does a recap. Then, she establishes *her objectives*, and goes to the meeting.

She comes back just before lunch, and takes a few minutes to do an *overview*, familiarising herself with the presentation of the document, checking if her objectives will be answered, or whether she should change these objectives now. Then she puts the report aside and goes to lunch.

Coming back, she expects a visitor. She does a *preview* in as short a time as possible, before receiving her visitor. When the visitor leaves Bel immerses herself in the report. She stops all distractions and reads (*inview*) and *reviews* the report.

HANDS-ON EXERCISES

☞ Take a document out of your in-tray. Flick through it. Be critical: can you tell what it is about? Can you find an Executive Summary or a Conclusion easily?

☞ Put the six-step approach to work with one long (over 500 pages) document.

☞ Go through your long-term filing system. Can you discard at least 50% of it?

☞ If you receive a document and you have no clear idea why, or you have difficulty in forming an objective to read it, ask 'Why has the sender sent it to me?' Be critical; do you need to read it at all?

☞ Practise recall patterns immediately after a meeting. Have you missed anything of importance? If you have, why?

Chapter 9
Applying the Six Steps to Reading Articles

A *FINANCIAL TIMES* ARTICLE

AN ARTICLE ON ECONOMICS

A FINANCIAL TIMES ARTICLE

The article in Figure 9.1 is taken from the *Financial Times* (December 1, 1993). Bel is interested in it and decides to apply her newly learned technique. Generally, newspapers, journals and magazines lack space which results in well-edited pieces. The fluff or irrelevancies – bumph – have been taken out. Bel can, therefore, combine Step 3 (Preview) and 4 (Inview). Bel feels that a Recap (Step 1) with a newspaper article is usually unnecessary.

Have you ever tried to write an article for publication? You are usually given a maximum number of words to write. You find it difficult to confine yourself to this limitation and send off your draft. The editor will send it back to you suggesting, amongst other things, that you drop this and that paragraph. You are aghast, thinking 'they' are pruning out your best bits! Trust them. The editor's experience is making your article more focused and easier for the reader to grasp your thinking.

STEP 1. RECAP

Having looked at the news section of the *Financial Times*, Bel selects this article because the future of the European air industry interests her.

STEP 2. SET OBJECTIVES

Has Bel set her objectives? Why does she want to read this article, beyond general interest? She must be precise and set herself a time limit. For example, can she, in ten minutes, outline the reasons for Airbus needing to restructure?

STEP 3. OVERVIEW

Bel is taking two minutes to look at the diagrams, which do not give her the information she seeks.

STEP 4. PREVIEW AND STEP 5. INVIEW

Bel is combining Previewing and Inviewing, in other words, she is taking four lines at a time, zig-zagging for paragraphs which do meet her objectives. She slows down to two

The Airbus consortium must restructure and rationalise if it is to compete with US airline manufacturers, says **Paul Betts**

Penalties for excess baggage

European dreams of taking on the world in commercial aerospace *can* fly, as Airbus has shown over the past 23 years. Yesterday, the European consortium celebrated one of its biggest coups against Boeing when it delivered the first of 50 Airbus A320 aircraft to United Airlines, one of its US rival's most prized customers.

But for all the pomp and ceremony at the handover, anxiety is growing among Airbus partners that their success in building high-technology airliners may have engendered a corporate dinosaur.

Mr Jean Pierson, the outspoken Airbus chief executive, sounded warning bells last month with one of the provocative throwaway phrases he likes to toss off between puffs at a Gitane cigarette. The Airbus system had now reached its "genetic limits", he said, and without change it was in danger of losing out to its American competition.

"Success is not eternal; unless we work on it we won't be able to meet the n w challenges facing our industry," added a close adviser.

Attempts to rationalise the consortium have failed to bring about significant change, largely because of political squabbling and industrial rivalries between the partners and their governments. But faced with the deepest postwar recession in the industry and growing competition from Boeing, the world's biggest aircraft manufacturer, time is running out for Airbus.

Like Boeing, Airbus has been hit by the prolonged slump in civil aviation and the financial difficulties of many customers. It has been forced to cut its production rate from 157 aircraft last year to 142 this year. Airbus now expects output to drop to 138 aircraft both next year and in 1995.

The consortium does not expect any significant recovery in new aircraft orders until 1995 or 1996. Although it still has a backlog of 701 aircraft, so far this year it has won only 30 new orders and suf-

governments diagnosed the trouble four years ago, when they set up a committee to recommend improvements in the Airbus system to make it more responsive to market forces. It led to a streamlining of the management and the appointment of a financial comptroller. But it stopped short of proposing the evolution of Airbus from a GIE into a public limited company.

Since that report, Airbus officials concede little significant progress has been made to overhaul the consortium. "There has been a lot of thought but little action to date," one admitted.

Some improvement has been achieved by focusing all final assembly and internal aircraft fitting to individual customer specifications for new Airbus programmes on one site rather than in two different countries. In the past, Airbus aircraft were assembled in Toulouse, flown to Hamburg for cabin fitting and flown back to Toulouse for delivery to customers. Now all A330 and A340 widebody aircraft are assembled and fitted in Toulouse, while the A321 narrowbody aircraft is completed in Hamburg.

A degree of competitive tendering on new aircraft programmes has also been introduced, but it has been restricted to competition between the fou partners in the

week to Lucas's Jamestown, North Dakota, facility to pick up aircraft cargo hold components and systems for just-in-time assembly in Seattle.

While paying lip service to the need to rationalise Airbus's production process and give the consortium an integrated company structure to control costs and become more responsive to market forces, the partners, for different reasons, are reluctant to take the plunge.

"The questions the partners should now be asking is whether it makes sense to have 10 manufacturing plants scattered around Europe and whether they are European enough to accept that production should be concentrated on the most cost efficient sites and perhaps, for some tasks, outside Europe," said a senior executive of one of the partner companies.

BAe has long campaigned for an Airbus public limited company but, as a French official pointed out, the UK partner has been as reluctant as the others to dig deep into his pocket to address the capital funding problems of setting up an independent company. Aerospatiale has come round to the idea of establishing an independent structure for Airbus, but it is also under pressure from its government not to rock the boat with any restructuring which could provoke the sort of social backlash caused by the recent Air France job cut proposals.

However, it is Deutsche Aerospace (DASA) which appears to be the biggest obstacle to any change. German ambitions to become a leader in the European aerospace industry have caused considerable ill feeling in the consortium. Other partners were angered by DASA's efforts to co-operate with Boeing on a very large aircraft project and its takeover this year of the Dutch Fokker regional jet manufacturer to strengthen its claim to lead all Airbus narrowbody programmes.

DASA has also been forced to

Commercial aircraft: the big fight

Orders, cancellations and deliveries

	1988	1989	1990	1991	1992	1993*
Orders	1,060	1,083	1,238	655	455	506
Cancelled	9	26	58	143	135	282
Net intals	1,049	1,707	1,175	399	320	43
Deliveries	511	506	570	822	769	400
Changes	+538	+1,201	+608	-463	-468	-346

*First 9 months

Backlog by manufacturer

	Backlog	%	Value ($bn)	%
Boeing	1,259	54.7	87.5	56.9
Airbus	701	30.4	50.8	33.0
MDC	217	9.4	12.8	8.3
Others	127	4.6	2.9	1.8
Total	2,304	100	154.0	100.0

Commercial aircraft delivery estimates

Boeing
Airbus Industrie
McDonnell Douglas

Figure 9.1 A *Financial Times* article

All four Airbus shareholders – Aerospatiale of France (37.9 per cent), Deutsche Aerospace (37.9 per cent), British Aerospace (20 per cent) and Casa of Spain (4.2 per cent) – acknowledge that their business partnership set up two decades ago under the structure of a French Groupement d'Interet Economique (GIE) has now served its purpose.

Simply put, the commercial success of Airbus, whose sales reached $8bn last year, is in danger of being undermined by the group's own corporate structure and complex work-sharing production system based in four countries.

"Airbus has worked well for a long time," said the head of one of the four partner companies. "We must not forget that Airbus has now taken 30 per cent of the world market, makes technologically advanced aircraft and has kept the pressure on Boeing."

For Airbus, he added, the risk was that, without change, success could quickly turn into decline, as had happened to McDonnell Douglas. "McDonnell Douglas was the clear number two after Boeing, but it did not invest sufficiently in building up a competitive product range and improving its production system. With only 10 per cent of the market, it has now been overtaken by Airbus," he explained.

All the partners recognise the challenge for Airbus is to transform what was initially a job and wealth creation consortium to compete against the dominance of the US manufacturers into an independent company, mature enough to rationalise and restructure, take hard political and social decisions, and stand on its own two corporate feet.

Under the French collaborative GIE system, the role of Airbus is to co-ordinate the production and design of aircraft and market the product range. It has no obligation to publish annual accounts; and a lack of financial transparency in a system where the shareholders are the main suppliers has made it almost impossible to calculate Airbus costs.

The partners and their respective A321 and A319, new derivatives of the 150-seat A320.

These limited adjustments have hardly begun to address the scale of productivity improvements Airbus must make to keep up with Boeing, the partners agree. In the beginning, Boeing was complacent about the competitive threat posed by Airbus. But when the European consortium started making significant inroads in the US market with big orders from old Boeing customers such as Northwest and United, Boeing reacted on several fronts.

It pressed the Washington administration to campaign against European government subsidies for Airbus, which led to last year's compromise trade agreement between Europe and the US on direct and indirect subsidies for new civil aircraft programmes. It launched a new 400-seat widebody twin-engine aircraft, the 777, to defend its dominant position at the top end of the market.

Most significantly, it launched an aggressive long-term cost reduction and productivity programme with a strong customer focus to remain number one in the business.

Boeing's target is to reduce costs by 25-30 per cent and halve its aircraft production cycle times by 1998

Boeing's target is to reduce costs by 25-30 per cent and halve its aircraft production cycle times by 1998. It already produces aircraft faster than Airbus. It takes Boeing about 12 months to complete a 737, while Airbus takes 15 months to build an A320, which competes directly against the 737.

"Today we can live with this three-month gap, but we will be at a competitive disadvantage if Boeing achieves its aim to produce a 737 in only six months by 1998," said a senior Airbus official. Reducing cycle times improves productivity and bears directly on costs. "The benefits of the modern technology we offer on our aircraft would be eaten up by the added inefficiencies of a cheaper aircraft," he added.

The partners believe Boeing will now fix industry targets and Airbus will have to keep up. "This will lead us eventually to change the structure, but simply turning Airbus into a limited company is no substitute for getting your processes right," said Mr Richard Lapthorne, BAe's financial director.

Standing on the Airbus stand at the recent Dubai air show, Mr Pierson rattled off a list of inefficiencies in the system: too much bureaucracy and too long decision times; too much duplication in research and development and in many production tasks; political pressures reflecting different national priorities of some partners and their governments; difficulties in rationalising the overall process because of differing labour and social regulations in the partner countries; the lack of financial flexibility to raise funds in the market and support aircraft sales because decisions have to be adopted unanimously by all four partners.

The convoluted system of how independent component manufacturers supply parts to Airbus is a classic example of inefficiency, says Mr Pierson. The UK Lucas Aerospace group supplies about 15 different components for Airbus aircraft. But none go directly to Airbus.

Instead, some parts are manufactured at Lucas plants in the UK, sent to the German partner for partial fitting, then back to the UK to BAe at Chester for assembly on the wing sets BAe builds for Airbus, before the completed wings are

The Airbus system has reached its 'genetic limits'; without change it might lose out to US competition

shipped out to Toulouse for final aircraft assembly. Other Lucas parts are made at the company's French subsidiary but also have to go via Germany before finding their way back to France.

"We would clearly prefer to supply direct to Airbus," says Mr Frank Turner, Lucas Aerospace's managing director. "You get a much better price, delivery and service the closer a component manufacturer is to his ultimate customer," he explains. In the US, by contrast, Boeing now sends a truck once a throes of deep restructuring. "At present the Germans are simply refusing any change to the Airbus structure," said a senior executive in one of the other partner companies. "And when we eventually all finally agree to change, it is important that no single partner should try to seize this situation to reinforce his position," he warned.

Although the timetable for turning Airbus into a public limited company is more uncertain than ever, the partners believe they can make a start by improving the efficiency of the existing system. For example, they are considering establishing an asset management organisation within Airbus to help finance and place used aircraft in the market.

The restructuring and consolidation of other parts of the European commercial aircraft industry could also provide an incentive for broader rationalisation at Airbus. Aerospatiale and BAe have been holding intense talks to try to merge their loss-making turboprop-eller businesses into a joint company. If negotiations succeed, it could help Aerospatiale transfer its turboprop activities from Toulouse to concentrate all operations there on Airbus assembly.

Ultimately, the test will be whether the partners are prepared to let Airbus fly loose with its own independent identity. In many respects, Airbus's reputation has outstripped that of its partners, although they still regard Airbus as one of their subsidiaries. "Unless you can actively form a company and genuinely run it for the sake of its shareholders, you'll always be second class to a company managed uniformly like Boeing," said another Airbus insider.

But prospects for such radical reform, at this stage, appear slim. The collapse last week of the ambitious Alcazar project by four European airlines (SAS, KLM, Swissair and Austrian Airlines) to merge their operations is a stark reminder of how easy it is for the foundations of European collaboration to crumble like a Tower of Babel.

Chart: Aircraft seating bands — Airbus / Boeing / McDonnell Douglas

Airbus: A319, A320, A321, A310, A300, A340, A330
Boeing: 737, 757, 767, 777, 747
McDonnell Douglas: MD-80, MD-90, MD-11

Seating scale: 100 122 132 150 183 224 274 335 400 500

Premium and economy class seating bands

Source: Paribas Capital Markets, Airbus Industrie

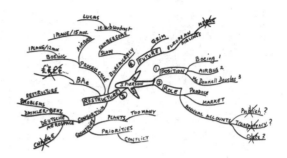

Figure 9.2 Mind Map® for *FT* Article on Airbus

fixations per line when the information answers her objectives. In this way, she spends four minutes reading this article. This article has roughly 2,000 words which gives her a speed of 500 words per minute.

STEP 6. REVIEW

She will check her comprehension, and make sure she has answers to her objectives. She wishes to retain this information and a Mind Map® will help her. Note that because of her objective, she has rearranged the information given in the article to suit her needs (see Figure 9.2). This personal involvement will reinforce long-term memory, as was discussed in Chapter 4. Altogether, she has spent nine minutes.

AN ARTICLE ON ECONOMICS

This example refers to 'Optional investing' taken from the finance pages of *The Economist* (see Figure 9.3).

1. RECAP

The article does not need a Recap because it is not a heavy, long document and the Recapping will come out automatically as it is read.

FINANCE

Optional investing

Can the theory of how to price financial options improve the way bosses invest their companies' money?

TALK to a company boss about financial options and he might smile at the prospect of exercising his generously priced share-options. Or shudder, maybe, at the reminder of the firm's incomprehensible hedging strategy. He will almost certainly not think about his recent decision to build a new widget factory, or to postpone the launch of the exciting new fax-cum-roller-blade that marketing says customers are baying for.

He should, however. For when he took those decisions, he probably obeyed the rules of financial-options pricing theory. Or so says a new book* by two economists, Avinash Dixit of Princeton University and Robert Pindyck of the Massachusetts Institute of Technology's Sloan School. In it, they attempt to integrate options theory and the traditional model of how firms decide where to direct their investment. Their merged theory, they say, better explains what really goes on inside firms, and clears up some real-world riddles the old approach left unsolved.

At business schools, managers learn to calculate the "net present value" (NPV) of a mooted investment. They forecast future profits, then discount them using a "discount rate" to reflect the higher value that money has today than in the future (usually the interest rate on government bonds plus a bit to offset the riskiness of the investment). That gives the present value of future profits. If this number is bigger than the present value of the costs of investing in the project—that is, the NPV is positive—then go ahead, says orthodox theory. Otherwise, think again.

All investment calculations rely on predicting uncertain future profits. But the traditional theory also assumes, implicitly, that investments are a now-or-never choice. That is unrealistic, say Messrs Dixit and Pindyck. Mostly, managers have some choice about when to invest. Waiting may mean missed opportunities. More often, in an uncertain world, it offers a valuable chance to learn more about the likely fate of the project.

The ability to delay an irreversible investment is like a financial "call option", say the two economists. The firm has the right, but not the obligation, to buy (invest in) an underlying asset (the profits from the project) at a price (the investment cost) at a future time of its choosing. This option has a value. When the firm makes the investment it exercises (or, in financial-market jargon, "kills") its option.

ECONOMICS FOCUS

It follows, then, that the cost of that killed option (the value of waiting for better information) ought to be included when calculating NPV. Before a project goes ahead, the present value of profits should exceed the investment costs by at least the value of keeping the option alive.

In the money

The price of a financial option is extremely sensitive to uncertainty about the value of the asset it gives the right to buy. So, too, is the value of what the authors call firms' "real options"—that is, untapped investment opportunities. Uncertainty about input costs, interest rates,

taxes and prices pushes up the real option "price" and increases the advantages to the firm of waiting.

It is profitable to kill a financial option as soon as the underlying asset value exceeds the option price plus investment cost—that is, when the option is what is known as "in the money". But financial-market traders mostly hold on to their options in the hope that they will yield even bigger profits by becoming "deep" in the money. The same logic applies to firms' real options.

Orthodox investment theory suggests that firms should invest in a project as soon as its NPV is positive. These two insights from option-pricing theory suggest something quite different: that it will often make sense for firms to invest in a project only when its NPV is very large.

In fact, that is what usually happens in practice. Most bosses do their basic NPV sums, but add in a margin to help them

feel comfortable. For instance, they may discount predicted profits using a "hurdle" required rate of return that is often two or three times the standard discount rate. Applying options-pricing theory to a big sample of typical business projects, the two economists found that such hurdle rates are perfectly sensible. However, the new "real options" theory allows bosses to set them on a more rational basis than gut instinct.

The theory also explains why firms often respond slowly to changes in tax, interest rates or demand—all of which, orthodox theory suggests, should elicit an instant response. Bosses are more interested in changes in uncertainty. Consider, for illustration, a government that cuts interest rates and taxes to boost investment, but as a result sows the seeds of longer-term economic troubles. It may actually increase uncertainty and cause firms to invest less.

The theory will be most useful in areas where the uncertainties are relatively apparent. The sums are already being churned over in the computers of some oil firms, for instance. There is one main risk in developing an oil field—a change in the oil price. Property developers, electric utilities and drugs companies are also investigating how to apply the theory in practice. It may work less well in, say, judging whether to invest in finding a cure for cancer, or in evaluating strategic decisions where long-term goals matter more than financial results.

Another problem is the theory's complexity: it has taken decades to persuade managers to use even the simple disciplines of the traditional NPV model. And, while the price of financial options is obvious, there will always be debate about the price of real options, which will be based on managers' assumptions about the future, not on market supply and demand.

Even so, the theory is likely to prove a big advance on the old NPV method. Though its aim is to improve company decision-making by showing how bosses can learn from financial markets, it can also help people in financial markets to understand firms better. Projects that a firm has not yet invested in may be at least as valuable to it as the ones that are going ahead—especially in a volatile market. Might bosses boost their firms' share price by telling analysts about all the lucrative things they are not doing?

....

* "Investment under Uncertainty", Princeton University Press, January 1994

Figure 9.3 Article from *The Economist* © The Economist, January 1994

2. OBJECTIVES

What is the theory? Can Bel grasp it in five minutes?

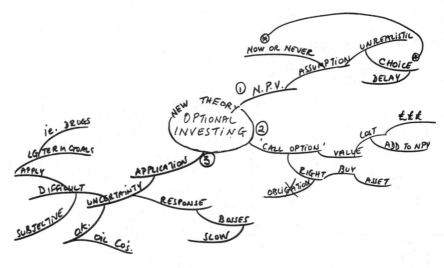

Figure 9.4 Mind Map® for Article on Optional

3. OVERVIEW

First Bel zigzags through the three columns, four lines at a time. It seems that one needs to start well into the article (at the bottom of the first column) as the first part is known background. Bel notes that this theory is proposed by two Americans.

4. REVIEW AND 5. INVIEW

As this article is in a magazine which usually is well edited, Bel can combine both these steps. The first three paragraphs, at zig-zagging pace, are of little use as they set the scene. The fourth, fifth and sixth paragraphs give the essence of the theory and these are read at cruising speed.

Now start at 'In the money' down to four paragraphs before the end. It gives background chat and justification that do not specifically meet Bel's objectives — they are read at zig-zagging speed.

The next three paragraphs (from 'the theory also explains' down to 'not on market supply and demand') elaborate on Bel's objectives — they are read at cruising speed. The last paragraph is not really relevant — a quick glance suffices.

6. REVIEW

The amount of information in this article normally would not merit notes being made, but Bel's Mind Map® is given in Figure 9.4 to demonstrate what somebody may like to do, perhaps to link it to other information.

Chapter 10
How to Present and Edit a Document

THE PRESENTATION OF DATA

THE PRESENTATION OF A PAGE

TIPS FOR THE EFFECTIVE PRESENTATION OF DOCUMENTS

FIRST IMPRESSIONS COUNT

FOUR STEPS TO EDIT A DOCUMENT

This chapter examines the presentation of documents. If you wish to be read, make documents attractive to the reader. It also offers a structured approach to editing documents. This last technique is adapted from the six-step approach described in Chapter 8.

THE PRESENTATION OF DATA

Figure 10.2 shows how *The Times* presented the Stock Market report until mid 1993. Figure 10.3 shows how *The Times* improved the presentation.

Which would you rather read? Which is easier?

THE PRESENTATION OF A PAGE

Spend five seconds looking at a typical book page, as set out in Figure 10.1:

Personal Development

All successful people have a common denominator: they have firmly established and clearly planned goals which they are moving towards. Only about 3% of people take the time to plan specific aims and objectives. It is therefore hardly surprising that success is not a common occurrence. You should start today on your road to being successful by planning your own future. Procrastination will only delay your goal achievement.

The art of 'Goal Setting' is worth learning and you will benefit from the time spent. Furthermore, by helping your new team members to set both short- and long-term goals you will be able to help them to formulate a sense of purpose and direction in their lives.

Goals need to be clearly written down, showing exactly what you and your colleagues wish to achieve. For instance, a specific amount of sales, or to qualify for promotion. Some goals may relate to being able to purchase household items, or being able to take a foreign holiday. Whatever the goal may be, it should always be in writing with a realistic time scale set for its achievement. Always remember to encourage your team members to be keen to share their aims and ambitions with you, so that you can help them achieve their goals. You should always target the challenges which must be met, and the action which must be taken to arrive at a chosen goal. This process will help you develop as a leader who is committed to goal achievement.

People react in a positive way to others who know where and why they are going. By setting goals you, in turn, motivate yourself with a sense of purpose. You know exactly where you are going, the vital ingredient for success.

As a motivated leader who wants to achieve success you must continually assess your goals. Sometimes it might be necessary to change direction, but not the goal. Flexibility in reaching your objective is important.

If you try one particular way and fail, do not give up. Look again and see if you can find a different route to success. Be receptive to new ideas and suggestions. There is always an alternative way to overcome a particular challenge. By helping your team members to achieve their goals you will also be reaching some of your goals.

People don't achieve success by luck or chance. When you look closely at successful people you will see a motivated person who is fully aware of where they are going, how long it will take, and what they need to do to get there.

Figure 10.1

- How does it appeal to you? How do you react?
- Would you want to read it?
- Why?

SUMMARY

STOCK MARKETS

New York
Dow Jones .... 2662.95 (+23.60)
Tokyo
Nikkei Dow .... 26029.22 (–18.95)
Hong Kong:
Hang Seng .... Market Closed
Amsterdam: Gen .... 318.0 (–3.2)
Sydney: AO .... 2150.2 (–12.9)
Frankfurt:
Commerzbank .... 2015.9 (+2.4)
Brussels:
General .... 5321.7 (–17.8)
Paris: CAC .... 428.7 (+2.7)
Zurich: SKA Gen ...... 589.70 (–2.9)
London:
FT.–A All-Share . 1146.69 (+2.71)*
FT.– "500" .... 1263.89 (+1.26)*
FT. Gold Mines .... 431.5 (–4.1)*
FT. Fixed interest .... 92.58 (–0.19)*
FT. Govt Secs .... 85.05 (+0.09)*

Closing prices   Page 23

INTEREST RATES

London: Bank Base: 10%
3-month Interbank 10½-10⅜%*
3-month eligible bills:10%-10¹₃₁%*
buying rate
US: Prime Rate 8¼%
Federal Funds 6⅞%
3-month Treasury Bills 6.23-6.24%
30-year bonds 97³₃₂-97½

CURRENCIES

London:	New York:
£: $1.6305*	£: $1.6305
£: DM2.5965*	$: DM1.8165
£: SwFr2.4360*	$: SwFr1.4985
£: FFr9.8727*	$: FFr6.0700
£: Yen231.76*	$: Yen142.45
£: Index:72.5*	$: Index:101.1*
ECU £0.701159*	SDR £0.794551*

GOLD

London Fixing:
AM $455.90 pm-$453.40*
close $453.50-454.00* (£278.25-
278.75*)
New York:
Comex $450.80-451.30

* Denotes Friday's trading price

Analysis	20	USM Prices	20
Gilt-Edged	20	Wall Street	20
Inv Trusts	20	City Diary	21
Foreign Exch	20	Econ View	21
Money Mrkts	20	Share Prices	23

❀ ❀ ❀ ❀

Figure 10.2 Stock Market report, *The Times* until mid
1993 © Times Newspapers Ltd. 1993

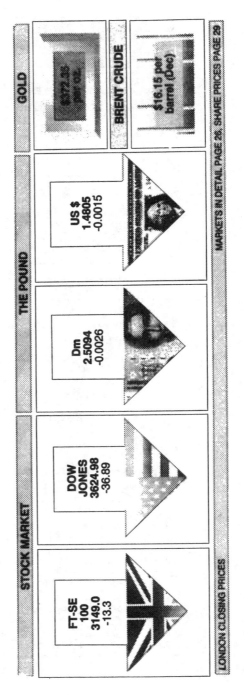

Figure 10.3 How *The Times* improved the Stock Market
report © Times Newspapers Ltd. 1995

Does the page have any appeal? Are you interested in reading it? Bel thinks lack of enthusiasm to read it may be due, in a large part, to the following:

- The lines are too long. Your brain has deduced that it will require a physical effort to read the page.
- Having to look for clues leading to important items in the text. The uniformity of presentation makes this search difficult.
- The impression of characterless bulk. The page is too full and lacks interest.

The same page could be presented as shown in Figure 10.4.

The Art of Goal Setting

Successful people have a common denominator. They are moving towards firmly established and clearly planned goals. Only about 3% of people plan specific aims and objectives for their life. Therefore it is not surprising that success is not a common occurrence in everyday life. You should start today to plan for success by planning your own future. Procrastination will only delay your goal achievement.

The art of 'Goal Setting' is worth learning and you will benefit from the time spent. Also, by helping your new team members to set both short- and long-term goals you will be able to help them to formulate a sense of purpose and direction in their lives.

How do you set goals?

Goals need to be written, showing clearly what you and your colleagues wish to achieve, for example, a specific amount of sales, or to sponsor a set number of people into the business, or to qualify for the company foreign conference. Some goals may relate to being able

---

to purchase household items, or being able to afford a
family holiday. Whatever the goal may be, it should
always be in writing with a realistic time scale set for its
achievement. Always remember to encourage your team
members to be keen to share their aims and ambitions
with you, so that you can help them achieve their goals.
You should always target the challenges which must be
met, and the action which must be taken to arrive at a
chosen goal. This process will help you develop as a
leader who is committed to goal achievement.

The benefits of goal setting

People react in a positive way to those who know where
they are going and why they are going there. By setting
goals you, in turn, motivate yourself with a sense of
purpose. You know exactly where you are going, the
vital ingredient for success.

As a motivated leader who wants to achieve success
you must continually assess your own and colleagues'
goals. Sometimes it might be necessary to change
direction, but not the goal: flexibility in reaching your
objective is important.

If you try one particular way and fail, do not give up.
Look again to see if you can find a different route to
success. Be receptive to new ideas and suggestions. There
is always an alternative way to overcome a particular
challenge. By helping your team members to achieve
their goals you will also be reaching some of your own
goals.

People don't achieve success by luck or chance. When
you look closely at successful people you will see
motivated people who are fully aware of where they are
going, how long it will take, and what they need to do to
get there.

Figure 10.4

TIPS FOR THE EFFECTIVE PRESENTATION OF DOCUMENTS

When you are writing a document do you ever pause to think about the reader? Indeed, do you want to be read? If you do, remember that what is unattractive to you will, probably, be unattractive to others. Well-presented documents can make the difference between successful sales and failure.

---

11 Tips for the Effective Presentation of Documents

✔ Reduce the number of words per line to a maximum of ten.

✔ Write, where possible, in double spacing.

✔ Have a maximum of one idea or subject per paragraph.

✔ Use different fonts to emphasise particular points in your message.

✔ In reports and similar documents, put a summary at the front.

✔ In documents over a few pages long, have an appropriate table of contents.

✔ Columns are easier to read than wide lines.

✔ Use appropriate icons to draw the reader's eye to key categories of information.

✔ Use diagrams, graphics and illustrations in preference to text.

✔ Introduce different subject sections with clear headings.

✔ Look at the document and ask yourself 'If I received this document would it invite me to read it?'

FIRST IMPRESSIONS COUNT

How often, when meeting someone for the first time, have you made up your mind about the person in the first five minutes? How quickly, as you browse in a bookshop, do you make up your mind about buying a book?

8. That's Not My Area

Exercise: Where do you hunt for ideas? What people, places, activities, and situations do you use to get new ideas?

I've asked many people this question. Here are some of their ideas.

Magic. Through the study and performance of magic, I've learned the power that certain symbols have when they are associated with one another. I've taken this knowledge and applied it to sales and product demonstrations.

Acting Class. From acting class I have been able to appreciate the impact that positive encouragement has on a person. I have seen some performances that were so bad I was embarrassed to watch. But the acting coach gave the person criticism in an encouraging way. As a result, these people were able to grow as actors. I think that there is a lesson here for many areas of life.

Family Trips. Whenever our family goes on vacation, I have made it a practice to take them on a tour through an operating plant to see how things are made and what procedures are used. We have seen sheet factories, record factories, distilleries, and ceramic factories.

Junk Yards. Going to a junk yard is a sobering experience. There you can see the ultimate destination of almost everything we desire.

Different People. I like to spend time with people whose value systems are different from my own. I like to see what's important to them, and that gives me a perspective on what's important to me.

Daydreaming to a Sound Effects Record. It really sets my mind free.

Figure 10.5 First Impressions Count

First impressions count. By how much?

The example in Figure 10.5 taken from Roger von Oech's clever and witty book on creativity, *A Whack on the Side of the Head* (4), demonstrates concern for the reader.

FOUR STEPS TO EDIT A DOCUMENT

 Case Study

Consider now the case of John, a surveyor in a large retail organisation. John has requested three independent architects (A, B and C) to tender for the design of a supermarket which is to be built. By the tender closing date each architect has responded, and John examines the tenders.

Architect A's tender is attractively and clearly presented. John can quickly find the key items he is looking for — a summary at the front, previous experience of this type of work, and costs. The architect has written the tender with John in mind and has clearly labelled each section of the bid. The two other tenders (B and C) are poorly arranged and it is difficult to locate information; the print is small and there is too much information per page, without clear headings. John will have to dig for the information he wants the hard way.

If you were John, what would your thoughts be now?

- *A favourable impression which increases the chances of success for Architect A?*

- *A supplier who has you in mind when tendering for a job will tend to keep your needs in mind if the job becomes theirs?*

- *Conversely Architects B and C do not seem to care about John's current requirements. Will they care in the future?*

All documents are written to sell something. (Otherwise what is the point of writing?)

If you were to build a new house, where would you start?

Would you first establish the kind of taps you wanted for the bathroom? Probably not. You might start with drawing an

outline picture of the whole house and garage. The picture will
have some key features. Either it will show a porch with pillars,
or a long bungalow or large top-to-bottom windows —
whatever you want. Then you might think of the materials
you want to use — stone, brick, wood, slate or thatch, and
insulation.

Once your house is designed you turn your attention to
fitting it out — what type of bathroom taps and kitchen sink —
and when it is built, to decorating it. In other words you
concentrate on the structure before getting down to the
details.

Editing a document requires a similar approach or frame of
mind. To edit a document apply a similar approach to the six
steps described in Chapter 8. But here you need only four
steps as shown in Figure 10.6.

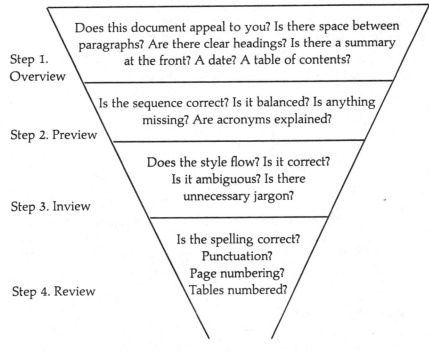

Figure 10.6 Four steps to edit a document

STEP 1

Flick through the *whole* document to gain a general impression, as you would do in a bookshop.

★ *If you are unhappy with what you see, send the document back to the author with your comments. She or he will need to correct the presentation before you examine the document more closely.*

STEP 2

Take a closer look, skimming about four lines at a time to gauge the sequence and the balance. If the document is to compare x, y and z, does it give equal space to each or space in proportion to the importance of each?

★ *If you wish to change the sequence, for example, put paragraph seven ahead of paragraph three, send the document to the author with your comment, before reading it carefully as in step three.*

STEP 3

Read carefully at your own speed (cruising speed); you are checking for style, that statements are factually correct, and that the document sets out its statements clearly and in a logical order. Try to delay correcting spelling and other small details until later.

★ *If you have many comments to make, send the document back to the author before proceeding to step four.*

STEP 4

Check all the typographical details.
  The benefits of the four-step approach are:

● At each step both editor and writer know where they stand and are less likely to make mistakes or invest a lot of work which is wasted by subsequent alterations.
● Each step meets a clear objective. The approach starts with a broad view and progressively moves towards the more detailed work.

● The editor's job is to ensure that the document is assembled in the most effective manner and proceeds logically towards its goal. He or she does this by comment and suggestion. The writer's job is to set down the facts (or fiction), following the editor's guidance, and to look after the details to produce a polished work. Editing a document does not mean rewriting it for a poor author. Editing can, therefore, teach a writer how to write better in future.

Bumph-free future . . .

I hope that the experiences of Ben and Bel have given you, the reader, some ideas on the question of bumph. But you will not have an automatic improvement in your bumph-handling ability unless you DO most of the exercises described here. Only a few minutes a day practice will soon turn you into an effective bumph disposer and an interesting information gatherer. Anything that you can do to streamline the amount of bumph that surrounds you is a step in the right direction.

The computer is entering our offices and homes more and more, and it too brings bumph problems. But the computer does bring one skill that no one person possesses, the ability to scan enormous numbers of records according to any selection instructions which have been fed into it. Some manufacturers have designed software that, in addition to recording minutes of meetings and notes about telephone conversations, will also pass on the information to the right people at the right time. If ever you are faced with the task of organising a large quantity of information, which much current legislation requires to be kept, a computer may be able to help you, but it cannot yet prune out the bumph.

Good luck! Start to have fun with the bumph, regarding it as a challenge with which you can play not as a serious impediment to your leisure, pleasure and work.

Bibliography

The following books are either referenced in the text ( ) or are recommended for further reading to provide you with new insights to stimulate your creativity in business affairs.

1. John Holt, *How Children Learn*, Penguin, 1967
2. Douglas R. Hofstadter, *Metamagical Themas: Questing for the Essence of Mind and Pattern*, Penguin, 1985
3. Frank Smith, *Reading*, Cambridge University Press, 1978
4. Roger von Oech, *A Whack on the Side of the Head*, Warner Books, N.Y., 1983
5. Shoshana Zuboff, *The Age of the Smart Machine*, Heinemann Professional Publishing, 1988
6. Alan McAuslan, *Dyslexia: What Parents Ought to Know*, Penguin, London
7. Anthony Smith, *The Mind*, Viking, London, 1984
8. The British Dyslexia Association, Church Lane, Peppard, Oxfordshire RG9 5JN
9. Kathryn Redway, *How to be a Rapid Reader*, National Textbook Company, Lincolnwood, Ill. USA, 1991
10. W. H. Bates, *Better Eyesight Without Glasses*, Grafton, 1979
11. A. R. Luria, *The Working Brain*, Penguin, London
12. J. Z. Young, *Programs of the Brain*, OUP, Oxford, 1978
13. Tony Buzan, *Use Your Head*, BBC Publications, London, 1955
14. Direct Mail Information Service, *The Letterbox File 1993*
15. A. V. Akro, B. W. Kernighan and P. W. Weinberger, *The AWK Programming Language*, Addison-Wesley, 1988
16. R. S. Wurman, *Information Anxiety*, Pan Books 1991
17. G. Nadler and S. Hibino, *Breakthrough Thinking*, Prima Publishing, 1990
18. Tony Buzan, *The Mind Map® Book*, BBC Publications, 1995
19. Mark H. McCormack, *What They Don't Teach You at Harvard Business School*, Bantam Books, 1984

Index

Anticipation   26, 77
Anxiety   51
Assertiveness   19
Attitude   19

Blockages   46ff
Brain, and memory   50
    comparison with computer
    38ff
Bumph   38, 40, 59ff, 107
    definition of   13
    log   60
Buzan, Tony   11, 55

Chunks   48, 52
Comprehension   21, 68, 74,
    86, 96
Computer   33ff, 63
Concentration   15, 68, 77
Conditioning   94, 101
Confidence   19
Consolidation   97
Cruising   133
Culture   37

Deadlines   48
Delegation   29, 45
Dickens, Charles   71
Distractions   77
Document presentation 123ff
Dynamics of reading   83ff
Dyslexia   79

Editing   131
Electronic text   14, 33
Empowerment   63
Eye movements   86
Eyes, resting   34, 98
Eyesight, better   26, 99

Fixation   87
Flexibility   69, 111
Franklin, Benjamin   105
Frequency   59

Goals (see also objectives
    22ff, 127
Grouping words   80, 86, 98
Guide, using a   80, 91ff,
    98
Gutting   44

Habits   74, 83
Hoover, J. Edgar   64

Imagery, see Visualisation
Improve, desire to   19
Information   43ff
    dissemination   62, 64
    technology   37
Insecurity   70
Interruptions   47, 56
Inview   108, 113, 115, 120

Keywords   55, 95

Meetings   16, 30ff
Memory   15, 49ff, 70
Merritt, D. L.   20
Miller, George A.   52
Mind Map®   55, 110,
   118, 120
Mnemonics   53
Motivation   85, 93, 98
Myths   68

Network   44
Notes (see also Recall
   patterns)   15, 109

Objectives   85, 96, 98, 100,
   104, 105, 106, 113, 115
Obligations   51
Overview   106, 113, 115

Pattern, of a book   103
   recall, see Recall Patterns
Peripheral vision   88
Presentation   123
Preview   107, 115
Priorities   29, 112
Procrastination   47, 56
Problems   59
Purpose   62

Reading   67ff
   on a screen   33ff
   speed   82ff
   strategy   13, 22ff

Recall (retrieval)   50, 52, 55
Recap   104, 115, 119
Recognition   21
Regression   86, 93, 98
Relax   19
Respond   22
Review   109, 113, 118, 121
Rhythm   94

Scanning   69, 107
Sensory assistance   80
Shape   20
Skimming   107, 133
Speed
   calculate   73
   maintaining   99
   variation   93
Subvocalisation   75
Systematic   105, 111

Technical documents   69
Time management   29ff, 112
Typeface   36

Unsolicited mail   42
Understanding see
   Comprehension

Visitors   49
Visualisation skills   76, 82

Writing on screen   35

HIGH INCOME CONSULTING

HOW TO BUILD AND MARKET YOUR PROFESSIONAL PRACTICE

TOM LAMBERT

"Lambert's book offers sound advice on how to stay one step ahead of the pack. In essence, he is a consultant's consultant."
The Independent

"Comprehensive and expert advice . . . specific, detailed and extremely practical. This book can be recommended with enthusiasm to anyone."
Alan Fowler, Personnel Management

Tom Lambert's comprehensive guide is based on twenty years' research on what the most successful consultants actually do, and is written to help readers build and sustain high quality and highly profitable professional practices. Even in these tough times, such practices are growing at nearly 30% a year.

In a period when an increasing number of newcomers are drawn to consultancy, the book provides proven skills and management consultancy models for direct application in a special 'toolkit'. And at a time when accreditation for the profession is under serious discussion, it will enable even the experienced advisor to learn the most practical and professional ways to maximise value to the client and to themselves.

Tom Lambert is an internationally recognised consultant. He was the first British consultant to operate in the USA by two bodies (CPCM, CPC) and has recently been invited by the National Bureau of Consultants to Management to develop an Accreditation Process for the profession to meet the needs of the international Common Body of Professional Knowledge.

£12.99 PB 1 85788 035 8 (Nov 1995)
324pp 234x156mm

THE 10 NATURAL LAWS OF SUCCESSFUL TIME AND LIFE MANAGEMENT

PROVEN STRATEGIES FOR INCREASED PRODUCTIVITY AND INNER PEACE

HYRUM W SMITH

"If you want to manage change and make the days and decisions of your life count, this is your owner's manual."

Denis Waitley, author of *The New Dynamics of Winning*

Hyrum W Smith has developed a system that goes far beyond what is usually considered "time management" to change not only how people plan their time, but also how they approach their lives. He shows you how to make the most of your time and life. And yes, he shows you how to obtain what the title promises - inner peace.

His unique strategy of planning, prioritising, and value analysis will enable you to organise your time and life in a *meaningful* way by:

- Determining the highest priorities in your life and what you value most

- Reevaluating what events you can and cannot control

- Establishing SMART goals to put life in line with values

- Getting rid of "time robbers"

- Using the ABC valuing system - a plan that works for getting things done

- A planning system now used by more than 2 million people worldwide

Hyrum W Smith is the co-founder, Chairman of the Board and CEO of Franklin Quest which sells the Franklin Day Planner and conducts management seminars throughout the world. He is an internationally known motivational speaker who has trained senior executives at Merrill Lynch, Dow Chemical, Kodak and dozens of other companies.

£14.99 HB 1 85788 019 6 · £9.99 PB 1 85788 075 7
240pp 234x156mm

COPING WITH DIFFICULT BOSSES

DEALING EFFECTIVELY WITH BULLIES, SCHEMERS, STALLERS AND KNOW-ALLS

ROBERT BRAMSON

"Original and deals with a real problem for many, many managers. The author devotes each chapter to a different kind of office beast. The breed includes ogres, fire-eaters, artful dodgers, power clutchers, scallywags, schemers and skunks. There is a lot of good advice about coping with difficult bosses and it is worth dipping in to see whether your particular problem is addressed."

Rosemary Stewart, The Independent

In *Coping With Difficult Bosses*, Robert Bramson offers practical and sympathetic advice on how to recognise, understand and take action to combat the behaviour of such bosses and to overcome the stress, frustration and misery which they cause.

Bramson's key is coping. He tells you exactly what you need to do when dealing with managers who buttress their own strength and power by demonstrating how weak or out of control you are. Their bullying techniques are effective because they force you to react in specific ways. Coping strategies break the cycle through the use of substitute responses.

Packed with real-life case studies of people who have successfully followed Robert Bramson's advice, the book makes fascinating reading as a study in personality types as well as a solution to a prevalent problem.

Robert Bramson is an internationally famous management consultant and behavioural scientist whose clients include IBM, Bank of America and Hewlett-Packard. His previous books have included the American bestseller *Coping with Difficult People.*

£9.99 PB 1 85788 028 5
172pp 234x156mm

JUST THE JOB

TAKE CONTROL OF YOUR CAREER FOR THE JOB YOU WANT

JOHN BEST

"Busy managers - redundant or otherwise - will welcome its checklists, 'prompts' and planning charts, which are interspersed with cartoon drawings."

Personnel Management

Whether your concern is -

- Career planning and management

- Starting out on the executive ladder

- Finding work after redundancy

- Returning after a career break

You can transform your prospects and self confidence with this tried-and-tested toolkit (over 3000 executives have used the draft version and their comments have helped to make the book more 'user friendly').

Readable, practical and comprehensive the book covers many new topics, including -

- Finding jobs

- Your sales brochure

- Psychometric tests

- Discovering yourself

This is the first wholly British guide to job search and career management.

John Best is a Director of Bennington Honour Ltd and now manages twenty-three training centres from Brighton to Gloucester serviced by some fifteen associates.

£9.99 PB 1 85788 034 X
152pp 246x189mm

ORDER FORM

Titles are available from all good bookshops, OR

SEND YOUR COMPLETED ORDER TO:

Nicholas Brealey Publishing Ltd Tel: +44 (0)171 430 0224
21 Bloomsbury Way   *Fax: +44 (0)171 404 8311*
London WC1A 2TH
UK

Or in Australia to Allen & Unwin Pty Ltd

Title	ISBN	Price	Qty	Cost
			Sub-total	
	Postage (UK or surface mail outside the UK)		+ £2.95	
	OR Postage Airmail (add £8.00 and delete £2.95 above)			
			TOTAL	

BY CHEQUE:

I enclose a cheque (payable to Nicholas Brealey Publishing) for £ . . . .

BY CREDIT CARD:

I authorise you to debit my credit card account for £ . . . .
My Access/Visa/American Express/Diners Club card number is:

Expiry date: . . . . .Tel no: . . . .

Cardholder's Name: . . . . .Signature: . . . .

Position: . . . . .Organisation: . . . .

Address: . . . . .Postcode: . . . .

Pro Forma Invoices issued on request: Please tick

Bulk Order discounts are available. Please call +44 (0)171 430 0224

If you do not wish to receive further information please tick this box